THE 'NEW' RULES OF ENGAGEMENT

A GUIDE TO UNDERSTANDING AND CONNECTING WITH GENERATION Y

BY MICHAEL MCQUEEN

THE 'NEW' RULES OF ENGAGEMENT
A GUIDE TO UNDERSTANDING AND CONNECTING WITH GENERATION Y

Copyright © Michael McQueen 2011
First published in 2007 by The Nexgen Group
Second edition printed in 2008
Revised and reprinted June 2009, April 2010
www.TheNexgenGroup.com

ISBN: 978-1-60037-717-4

Cover Design by Tim Matta of Hammer + Tongs Creative
www.hammerandtongs.net.au

Edited by Clear Communications
www.clearcommunications.net.au

Typesetting and layout by Imperial Metric
www.imperialmetric.tv

The moral right of the author has been asserted.

Library of Congress Control Number: 2009937705

DEDICATED TO WILLIAM J. MCQUEEN

(1953-2004)

A wonderful father, wise mentor and best friend

CONTENTS

ACKNOWLEDGEMENTS

At the age of 22, I felt that I had a lot to teach. I started The Nexgen Group with the bold notion that I knew everything necessary to equip and prepare students for their career and future.

Instead, I found that I had a lot to learn!

Since those early days, the breathtaking growth in the scope and influence of Nexgen's work has never ceased to amaze me. I could never have imagined that within a few short years we would be operating at an international level and touching the lives of over 20,000 young people each year. I certainly never expected that the lessons I learned in those formative years would one day form the foundation of a book that would reshape the way governments, corporations, schools, parents, hospitals, churches, the police and even the military approached their work with young people.

However, like any success story, the Nexgen journey is marked by the input of many people to whom I am deeply indebted.

My first thanks must go to Lyn Camp and the Careers Advisers Association of New South Wales. Without your assistance, ideas and encouragement, I would have never got off 'Go'!

I am also very grateful to numerous individuals from the New South Wales Department of Education and Training, with a special mention to Hanna Kemp from the Western Sydney Regional Office. Your vision, superb networking skills and generosity with time and input were instrumental factors in Nexgen's early growth and evolution.

Of the many others who have played significant roles, I especially want to acknowledge Sam Haddon, Carlie Boyton, Chris Stewart, Phyllis Devereaux, John and Denise Hargreaves, and Graham Agnew. In different ways each of you has been a key influence in both my business and my life.

Thanks also to my newest parents, Ross and Nessie. Your limitless encouragement and belief in me has been, and remains, invaluable.

To my wonderful Mom – you are an inspiration! I am so proud of you and thank you for the love and example that you and Dad have shown me in life. I am blessed to have had parents who modeled what it meant to sacrifice for and invest in the next generation.

A big thank you also to my long-suffering and exceptional assistant Liz. Your thoroughness, generous nature and sense of humor are more appreciated than you could ever know. You are a gem!

Above all, my most heartfelt thanks go to my beautiful wife, Hailey. Thank you for your patience as I spent endless days locked up writing and for your continued encouragement when I wanted to quit. Your love, support and belief gives me the courage to become the man you deserve. I love you.

Finally, thanks to the many hundreds of audiences to whom I have had the privilege of presenting in recent years. This book is the culmination of the lessons you taught me as I endeavored to teach you.

INTRODUCTION

You already know each other well – or do you?

You and they are different. You know this but perhaps don't know why. The world you have always known seems so different to theirs.

They have a hard time imagining a home without a computer for everyone over the age of four. You have a hard time understanding how your four-year-old niece can program the hard disk recorder you find almost impossible to use.

They ask what going to a library used to be like 'in the old days' before the internet answered every conceivable question. You wonder when *Google* became a verb.

They speak of PDAs, DVDs, MP3s and iPods. You are still trying to figure out what LOL means.

They wonder if perhaps the Cold War occurred during the last ice age. You remember when Reds lurked under the bed.

They have no idea what a broken record is or what you mean when you say they sound like one. You remember when cassette tapes were revolutionary.

Who are 'they'? Good question. They go by many names – 'The Millennials', 'The Net Generation', 'Generation Y2K', 'Generation Why', 'Echo Boomers' and even 'The Sunshine Generation'.

However, the name by which they are most commonly known is 'Generation Y'.

Born in the 1980s and 1990s, this group of 71 million young Americans is one of the most widely misunderstood and misrepresented generations of recent times.

First named and categorized by a journalist in *Advertising Age* in the early 1990s,[1] Generation Y has to this day remained a subject of great fascination and intense scrutiny. Countless books, research papers and

"PARENTS, TEACHERS AND EMPLOYERS AUSTRALIA-WIDE FIND THEMSELVES TRYING TO CONNECT WITH A GROUP OF YOUNG PEOPLE THEY SIMPLY DON'T UNDERSTAND."

newspaper articles have been written in an effort to understand where they have come from, what they think, and how to connect with them.

Much of this material has emerged as a result of the needs of business. The record-breaking unemployment figures experienced prior to the Global Financial Crisis (GFC) coupled with an aging workforce and skill shortages have led corporations to invest tens of millions of dollars in an attempt to understand how best to recruit, manage and retain Gen Ys.

Advertising companies have also shown a keen interest in profiling and targeting this group – after all they are the most prosperous youth market in history.[2]

Indeed, the concept of 'engaging Generation Y' has become a buzz topic in recent years. As a speaker in this field, my travels have allowed me the opportunity to work with thousands of teachers, parents and business owners who deal with this generation on a daily basis. Just like you, these are the everyday people who are on the front line when it comes to responding to and connecting with young people.

In all these discussions I tend not to hear the rhetoric that some sociologists throw around in relation to this group. I sadly hear relatively few upbeat stories of parents, teachers and employers finding this generation a joy and pleasure to interact with.

Instead, the words I hear said most often by those who work with Generation Y are 'frustrating' and 'confusing'. In so many areas of interaction, older generations are exasperated by a generation that seems disinterested, disloyal, disrespectful and self-centered.

Parents, teachers and employers the world over are finding themselves trying to connect with a group of young people they simply don't understand. They speak of this generation's brash self-confidence, impatient arrogance, and unfocused flippancy, and are left asking one question: 'What do we do with them?'
This book is designed to help you find an answer to that question for yourself. I can't offer you the 'magic pill' or give 'three steps to instant engagement'. What I can offer you are ideas, insights and understanding.

Having presented to and coached over 80,000 Gen Ys (and being a member of this generation myself), I want to help you get inside the heads of this group so you can better understand them.

That said, I think it is inadequate to simply stop at the point of understanding. There are a number of great books with a specific focus on *understanding* different generations. Although valuable in its own right, I believe this approach is too limited.

While understanding is a key part of developing empathy, true empathy will always inspire action. That is, to know and not to do is not to know at all. Understanding without a resultant action is like the person who has seen all the World Vision advertisements on television, has developed a great sense of empathy for the poor of the developing world, but has never made a donation.

Real awareness and understanding *must* prompt a response. In other words, how will understanding Generation Y help you better connect with them.

I find that what teachers, parents and employers want more than anything else are practical strategies that will lead to *engagement* with young people. They want to engage *with* this group and get a sense of engagement *from* them in return.

Some descriptions that are commonly used when you examine the word *engage* in the dictionary describe the concept perfectly:

- *to occupy the attention or efforts of a person or persons*

- *to attract, hold fast or involve*

- *to interlock with or become connected to*

Put simply, engagement is about three things: commitment, attraction and connection.

My hope is to equip you with understanding, tools, strategies and ideas that will enable you to powerfully engage Generation Y.

This book is divided up into three broad sections, each designed to help achieve this end:

Section one will clarify what a generation is, and start by expanding some of the labels that are used to classify groups of people by their age. I hope to give you an insight into how the era in which you were born has shaped your world view, and in turn, how this world view affects the way you relate to others.

Section two will look at a number of significant areas of 'Paradigm Rift' that exist between generations. Specifically, I will highlight Generation Y's perceptions and mind-set in comparison with an established societal perspective.

Finally, in section three I will highlight a number of strategies or 'rules' for engaging Generation Y whether you are an educator, an employer or parent of this group.

So hold on for the ride. You may come across some radical new ideas in the pages ahead that challenge the way you think. But remember; minds are like parachutes… they work best when they are open!

gen·er·a·tion

[jen-*uh*-rey-sh*uh* n]

noun

The entire body of individuals born and living
at about the same time who share similar
ideas, problems and attitudes.

WHAT IS A GENERATION?

1

1
CHAPTER ONE
SETTING THE SCENE

You could be forgiven for thinking that the idea of classifying and studying generations was something new. You may be tempted to dismiss the whole notion as the latest fad of overzealous managers and marketers keen to find a competitive edge. Maybe you are skeptical of the language and labels used and wonder whether breaking people into categories based on their birth year is nothing more than a simplistic and patronizing overgeneralization designed to 'box' people.

If you fall into any of the above groups, you are not alone.

You may, however, be surprised to learn that the study of generations goes back as far as the Greek historian Cicero and the ancient writers Heraclitus and Homer. The Chinese philosopher Lin Yu-t'ang and the Hebrew writers of the Old Testament also placed a great deal of emphasis on the significance and meaning of generations.

In recent decades the emphasis that social researchers have placed on the study of generations has increased dramatically. I would suggest that there are two reasons for this.

Firstly, information is more readily available in our modern age than in centuries past. The quantitative data that forms much of the basis of this area of sociology is being collected and analyzed now more than ever before.

Secondly, and more importantly, the impact of generational change was significantly greater in the 20th century than in any previous era. After all, the difference between someone born in 1840 and someone born in 1880 would be nowhere near as significant or profound as that between people born in 1940 and 1980.

"WHAT WAS CONSIDERED RISQUÉ ONE HUNDRED YEARS AGO COULD NOW BE SEEN AS PRUDISH."

What a difference one century has made. With the increased pace of technological and social change, the gap between generations has never been greater.

In his book, *Mind the Gap*, Graeme Codrington picks up on this point, saying:

In the 'good old days', before the dawn of the 20th Century, there was no need for a formal generational theory in order to get a handle on the mindsets, perceptions, value systems, attitudes and opinions of the era. Time moved slowly, change was measured and almost imperceptible. When a grandparent held her infant grandchild in her arms, she could safely imagine that the life of that child and its future would be much the same as they had been for her.[3]

It goes without saying that society's collective views on morality, family and behavior have evolved enormously over the course of the 20th century. Our collective values have fundamentally shifted during this period. What was considered risqué one hundred years ago could now be seen as prudish.

Before we dive into a discussion about the impact of these changes and what they mean for you as you relate to Generation Y, let's define some basic terms and concepts.

Firstly, 'generation' is simply a term that describes a group of people that are born at about the same time. The Oxford Dictionary defines a 'generation gap' as the variance in opinion between those of different generations.

'Generational theory' is the area of sociology that deals specifically with mapping, classifying and understanding the characteristics of different generations and how the gap between them is expressed.

Typically, a generation represents a period of roughly twenty years. However, generations are sometimes grouped together due to a set of common influences and characteristics. For example, the 'Builder' generation (see below) is actually a combination of two cohorts – the 'GI' generation and the 'Silent' generation. Many sociologists group them together for ease of analysis.

Broadly speaking, if we look at the 20th century there are five main generations:

NAME	BIRTH YEARS
The Builders	Early 1900s – Mid-1940s
The Baby Boomers	Mid-1940s – Mid-1960s
Generation X	Mid-1960s – Early 1980s
Generation Y	Early 1980s – Late 1990s
Generation Z	Late 1990s – ?

While there is often debate as to where the boundaries between generations should be placed, the labels and years shown above represent those that are most widely accepted.

However, at this point it is worth stating that the labels themselves are not important – their significance lies in what they represent.

To fully understand what makes each generation unique we must take into account many factors. These can include the significant events, social norms, shared experiences, financial backdrop and cultural climate that existed in the formative years of each group.

Eminent US psychologist Lawrence Kohlburg suggests that a child's opinion of what is right, wrong and normal is predominantly formed by the age of ten.[4] Therefore, when profiling behaviors and mindsets, it is necessary to identify the influences at play in the formative years of a specific generation. Based on this, we can then compare generational mindsets, develop greater understanding and begin to communicate and engage with each other more effectively.

2 CHAPTER TWO
LIMITATIONS
AND BOUNDARIES

Despite the inherent value in developing an understanding of other generations, it would be naïve to ignore the limitations and dangers that exist when we define and characterize people based on the year that they were born.

There are, in fact, some who would dismiss the basic premise of generational theory altogether. In his book *Gangland*, Mark Davis argues that 'generalizationalism' is merely a tool used by those in power to ridicule young people in order to assert the role of being cultural and economic gatekeepers.[5] In stronger language still, US author and editor of *Slate* magazine David Plotz describes the process of generalising about generations as completely 'bogus'.[6]

I would, however, argue that such perspectives are both largely ill-informed and misguided. Having spent countless hours sifting through and studying some of the most current research available in this field, I would argue that there is certainly a relevance and validity to the profiling of generations.

I have witnessed firsthand the 'light-bulb moments' that occur when people suddenly see the impact of a generational background on mindsets, behavior and communication.

In the interests of best analysis, however, I do acknowledge three limitations to generational theory.

Firstly, it is important to be clear that a person's generation is only one factor in our understanding of human behavior. Factors such as culture, gender, nationality, personality and religion are integral parts of a person's behavioral make-up and must not be discounted or overlooked. That said, I have found that the influences of culture and ethnicity are playing a lesser role in shaping today's youth than they have in the past. This younger generation tends to be incredibly consistent around the world – the Gen Y phenomenon is indeed a global one. In my interactions with young people from the bustling streets of Seoul or New York City to villages in rural Uganda, there is an emerging worldwide youth culture that transcends ethnic or national boundaries in an unprecedented way. Young people around the globe are on the same social networking sites, listening to the same music and watching the same movies. While the labels attributed to Gen Y may change from country to country,[7] the underlying influences shaping young people do not.

> "EXCEPTIONS DON'T INVALIDATE THE RULE, THEY HELP TO DEFINE IT."

Secondly, generational theory should always be viewed as *descriptive* rather than *prescriptive*. To this extent, I agree with Mark Davis: generational theory is underpinned by broad generalizations. These generalizations, while helpful in describing identifiable patterns of behavior within a cohort, should not necessarily be interpreted as typical of a whole group.

You will undoubtedly be able to identify certain characteristics within yourself that don't neatly fit into the generational mold from which you are *supposed* to have come. That's okay – exceptions don't invalidate the rule, they help to define it.

It would perhaps be helpful to approach this book with the same mindset you would if reading *Men are from Mars, Women are from Venus*. In this revealing and landmark work, Dr John Gray never intended to specify what *all* men and *all* women were like. If that was what you were looking for you probably wouldn't have read past page four! Rather, by using everyday situations and examples, he was able to describe what *most* men and *most* women are like.

That is precisely what generational theory aims to do: highlight and examine the patterns and trends of the significant majority in a cohort. However, we must recognize that there will always be a place for diversity and non-conformity.

This leads me to the third limitation of generational theory: the labels and categories we use should not serve as something that we can hide behind or use as an excuse. To say, 'I'm a Baby Boomer, so I demand your respect' or 'I'm a Gen Y so I don't automatically give respect' would be an inappropriate use of generational insight. Identifying the characteristics of our own generation and the nuances of others should ideally *empower* us to connect across the generation gap rather than provide an excuse for why conflict is inevitable.

As we take an in-depth look at the five main generations of the 20th century, there are two factors we must consider:

1 INFLUENCES

What were the era-specific factors that shaped each generation?

As the old saying goes, people really do resemble their times more than they resemble their parents.[8]

2 CHARACTERISTICS

Based on these influences, what are some of the resultant characteristics and mindsets specific to each generation?

With those questions in mind, travel back with me to the beginning of last century, to the days when the automobile was a new invention, Charlie Chaplin was a rising star, and the sinking of the *Titanic* stunned the world.

Let's meet a generation known as the Builders.

3

CHAPTER THREE
THE BUILDERS

Born during the first four decades of the 20th Century, the Builders were a pioneering generation who, as their name suggests, built much of what we take for granted in modern society.

They were the first children to grow up under the protection of child labor legislation and were the first adolescents to receive the label 'teenagers'.[9]

This was a generation who boldly challenged the boundaries of human endeavor and achievement. Their heroes, Winston Churchill, Mahatma Ghandi and Superman, reflected the self-discipline, fierce courage and deep patriotism for which this generation would become known.

For much of the Builders' working lives, the Industrial Revolution was at its peak. Factories, production lines and all-powerful companies dominated the work and social landscape.

The Builders' childhood was one of dramatic extremes – the Roaring Twenties and the Great Depression; the 'war to end all wars' and the one that followed.

Indeed, the First and Second World Wars profoundly shaped the way this generation saw themselves and others. Some lingering effects of war are still evident in the Builders to this day. My grandfather, for instance, will still think twice before buying a product that bears the sticker 'Made in Japan'.

It could be said that the Builders grew up in an era so far removed from the modern age that it may as well have been another planet.

This fact became startlingly clear to me recently as I walked down the main street of Parramatta, a foundational suburb west of Sydney, Australia. In a rush between meetings, I was hurriedly checking my voicemail when I caught the tail end of a fascinating conversation taking place just a few steps behind me.

Tuning in just enough to be able to hear without looking as if I were eavesdropping, I heard an elderly lady speaking excitedly to her granddaughter.

This lady, clearly of the Builder generation, was describing the main street of Parramatta as it looked in the time of her youth. She pointed to the classic old buildings whose renovated facades still stood proudly. She described the narrow dirt streets, the corner where a young boy used to sell the newspaper and spoke of the old farm across the river, now a sprawling housing development.

As she described the scene of that same street eighty years before, I tried to imagine just how different things must have looked. I wondered what it was like before cars, glass towers and traffic lights dominated the streetscape. It was at this point that the elderly lady said something I will never forget.

'Do you know,' she said, 'when I was six years old and we moved here from interstate, the journey was not anywhere near as fast as it is nowadays. In fact, it took us nearly three and a half weeks!'

The granddaughter was clearly surprised by this.

'Are you serious? How come it took you so long?' she asked innocently.

The grandmother explained. 'Well, we didn't come by car or plane like you would now, we came by horse and carriage!'

I was stunned. What an incredible thing! There I was checking my voicemail on a space-age phone which I accept unthinkingly as a normal part of life and yet walking down the street just a few metres behind me was a woman who had seen and known a world so unlike today's that I could scarcely imagine it.

The Builders certainly are the product of a different era.

CHARACTERISTICS OF THE BUILDER GENERATION

1 DUTIFUL

Sparked by the dire threat of war on a global scale, this generation exhibited a fierce nationalism and collective spirit.

When the call to arms came, those of the Builder generation dutifully fell into line, marching off to distant lands to fight for their country and the greater good. Their sense of submission to authority and 'knowing one's place' was reason enough to risk life and limb – an attitude firmly woven into the psyche of this generation.

"THE BUILDERS GREW UP IN AN ERA SO FAR REMOVED FROM THE MODERN AGE THAT IT MAY AS WELL HAVE BEEN ANOTHER PLANET."

During a recent speaking tour of Australia's Northern Territory, I had the chance to visit our equivalent of the Arlington War Cemetery in a town called Adelaide River. Walking around the well-maintained lawns of this proud national monument, I was struck by how many of the headstones bore inscriptions that would rarely be found in more modern cemeteries. Rather than describing the deceased in glowing, warm and personal tones, the bold epitaphs at Adelaide River reflected the sense of duty that inspired so many of the soldiers who had given their lives on the battlefield. Many of the headstones simply read – 'His Duty Nobly Done'.

Rotary International, an organization popularized by this generation, bears a motto that aptly describes the attitude of a Builder – *Service Above Self.*

2 FRUGAL

Defined as *'being economical in use or expenditure; prudently saving or sparing; not wasteful'*, frugality is a hallmark of the Builders.

Having grown up with war-time food rationing, this generation knows the value of things. 'Waste not, want not' is their motto.

You don't have to look far to see evidence of how this mentality has pervaded most areas of their lives, even to this day. For instance, the point at which a jar of peanut butter is officially, definitely and absolutely finished varies greatly depending on whether you are a Builder or a Gen Y.

For a Gen Y the jar is finished when the effort required to extract the remaining peanut butter outweighs the perceived value of the exercise. They may make a token effort to scrape out the jar but will just as happily throw it in the bin and buy a new one. After all, peanut butter only costs $2, so why bother wasting valuable time with the old jar.

A few days later a Builder parent or grandparent is shocked to discover that someone has prematurely thrown out the peanut butter without realising what they have wasted. Assuming there has been some mistake they rescue the jar from the bin, take it back inside and proceed to scrape enough peanut butter for another five or six sandwiches from the 'empty' jar.

Then, once the jar is *officially* finished I am sure you can guess what happens next…

That's right! The label is removed, the jar is washed out and it becomes a new home for other precious resources – jam, pickles, nuts, bolts, screws, paperclips, elastic bands – the list goes on! Next stop for the jar? It goes into a cupboard or the garage, of course, where it will remain till the day when its contents are needed.

Have you seen this or a similar scenario played out in your own home? Chances are you have – and this is generational theory in action.

Builders will go to great lengths to make sure nothing is wasted. This is not because of some genetic disposition or commitment to the environment, but rather the logical response of a generation who grew up with rationing during the war. Being wasteful was at least inappropriate and possibly even immoral. This goes a long way towards explaining why a Builder will toast moldy bread rather than throwing it out and darn ten-year-old socks rather than buy a new pair from Target.

My grandma typifies the thrifty nature of a Builder.

As one of five boys, buying Christmas presents for my brothers and I was always an expensive affair – unless you happened to be innovative like Grandma.

One year her Christmas present for my brothers and I arrived in the mail. We opened the parcel and looked inside, excited to discover that she had sent us a huge box of chocolates! Upon closer examination, however, it became clear that this box of chocolates had been opened and some of its contents had been eaten!

While we thought this was a little odd we dutifully did what all grandchildren must do – we called Grandma to thank her for her kind gift thinking little more of it.

A few months later, at a family gathering, my father had the chance to ask Grandma what had happened with the box of chocolates she had sent us. Her explanation of the chain of events went something like this:

Having gone to the post office and waited in the line it finally came time for her to be served. Grandma approached the counter and handed her parcel to the lady behind the desk. Everything was going as expected until the post office clerk placed the package on the scales. Grandma went on to describe her shock when the weight of the package pushed it just into the next price bracket, meaning it would cost substantially more to post. She immediately demanded the package back and, in front of everyone waiting in the line, she opened the parcel and the enclosed box of chocolates, poured some into her hand and hastily ate them. Asking the lady behind the counter to try again, she kept eating chocolates till the package weighed in just below the upper limit of the cheaper price category!

Modern-day grandparents, predominantly Boomers, are often shocked when they hear this story. It seems today that no expense is too great for a grandchild. Grandparents try to outdo and outspend themselves and each other in an effort to make sure that the grandchildren are thoroughly spoilt.

My grandma, however, recounts that morning at the post office with something approaching a sense of pride. For her generation, saving money at any cost is an admirable pursuit.

3 STOIC

The ancient Stoics held the belief that, by mastering passions and emotions, it was possible to overcome the discord of the outside world and find peace within oneself. The Builders lend themselves to such a philosophy. With a heavy reliance upon rational logic at the expense of emotion, they tend to approach everything from the way they express themselves to the way they face adversity with the notion of keeping a 'stiff upper lip'.

> "BUILDERS FIRMLY BELIEVE THERE IS A RIGHT AND PROPER WAY OF DOING MOST THINGS IN LIFE."

This in part explains why Builder men are often described as having an emotional 'constipation' that is not shared by their sons and grandsons. Younger generations who have grown up with *Dr Phil* simply wish their fathers and grandfathers would show more openness, affection and emotion. For many older men, however, relating in such a way would be considered uncomfortable and inappropriate.

4 PROPER

Builders firmly believe there is a right and proper way of doing most things in life. 'Proper' is defined as conforming to an established standard of behavior or manners. As such, there is a correct way to speak, to cross one's legs, to drink one's tea and to write a formal letter. Decorum is the name of the game.

It is not unusual for a Builder to don a coat and tie simply to go down to the corner store to buy the weekend paper. This is, after all, the appropriate way to dress when going out in public. They see younger generations wandering around wearing ugg boots and tracksuit pants and ask, 'What's wrong with today's youngsters?'

Just as the post-war world was settling back into normality and life was becoming predictable again, the birthing pains of the next society-wide upheaval were being felt. A new generation was on the way – a generation that would change the world forever. This generation's name? The Baby Boomers.

4
THE BABY BOOMERS

Born between the mid-1940s and mid-1960s, the Baby Boomers first received their name in Landon Jones's bestseller from the 1970s, *Great Expectations*.[10]

Upon returning from World War II, soldiers and their sweethearts were determined to make up for lost time. Undeniable evidence of their impassioned resolve was to be seen nine months later as the children of a post-war celebration began entering the world.

Almost overnight we witnessed a demographic explosion unlike anything the world had seen before. Hospitals ran out of maternity wards, baby food manufacturers couldn't keep up with demand and schools didn't have enough classrooms.

Boomers were born into a jubilant and prosperous society that had just endured and overcome the overwhelming challenges posed by the Great Depression and two World Wars.

While Boomers themselves are not old enough to remember World War II, the attitudes prevalent in its closing stages certainly carried through into all areas of society. Teamwork, commitment, persistence and victory became core foundations for the collective psyche of a new generation – particularly in the West.

Television had a massive impact on the childhood years of a Boomer. More than ever before, it meant that many of a child's formative influences came from outside the home. The Boomers grew up with television and it, in a sense, grew up with them.

"WHILE ONLY 0.5% OF U.S. HOUSEHOLDS HAD A TELEVISION SET IN 1946, THIS NUMBER HAD RISEN TO A STAGGERING 90% BY 1962."

Consider this: while only 0.5% of U.S. households had a television set in 1946, this number had risen to a staggering 90% by 1962.[11]

While the Boomers may have grown up watching iconic shows like Father Knows Best and Leave it to Beaver, they started to question the world they saw on television as they moved into adolescence. This process of questioning and challenging the status quo became a driving force behind what would later become known as the Swinging 60s.

Graeme Codrington describes the Boomers' burning of their bras, flags and draft cards as symbolic of their rejection of many of the traditional ways of doing things and of the authorities that enforced the rules. He suggests that the more this generation learned about the government the more they distrusted it. Their war cry of 'don't trust anyone over 30' pointed to a widespread cynicism and suspicion, not just of institutions, but of the perceived corruption within them.[12]

Anti-war moratoriums gave the Boomers a sense of purpose and collective strength that, ironically, their parents had found in fighting a war.

The Boomer-driven revolution of the 60s was felt on the home front as well. Traditional roles and expectations around gender were challenged like never before. First introduced in late 1960, the contraceptive pill was described by some as an invention with social significance equivalent to the steam train or the telephone. The new freedom and control that the pill afforded women coincided with the rise of the feminist movement. The combined influence of these factors changed life for women (and men) in profound and lasting ways.

CHARACTERISTICS OF THE BABY BOOMERS

1 OPTIMISM

Boomers exhibit an upbeat optimism which is, in part, a product of the many great feats of human endeavor and perseverance they witnessed while growing up. This generation saw Roger Bannister break the four-minute mile, Edmund Hillary conquer Mount Everest and man do the unthinkable – walk on the Moon!

The sky is the limit

Every cloud has a silver lining

What the mind can conceive and believe it can achieve

These and many other phrases have been made popular by the Boomers. After all, the self-help and motivation industry was largely started by, and for, this generation.

Optimism tends to be such a hallmark of Baby Boomers that you can often tell very quickly if a Boomer runs an office simply by virtue of the fact that somewhere on a wall will be a framed poster featuring a serene photo with a motivational quote beneath it. These posters, like the coffee mugs and mouse pads that go along with them, are symbolic of the optimistic, positive and upbeat mentality of many Baby Boomers.

2 CAREER-FOCUSED AND PROSPEROUS

With their dreams of a social revolution largely unrealized, the 1970s saw the Boomers move from being rebellious idealists to a hardworking middle class eager to take the reins of society.

Many Boomers settled down and directed their ambition and energy into career advancement. Ironically, the last three decades have seen Boomers assume positions of influence and leadership in the institutions they once riled against.

Aspiration has not been limited simply to the vocational realm but also the material. Many Boomers have got keeping up with the Joneses down to a fine art.

This is certainly a generation with significant financial clout. Figures released in 2009 indicated that Boomers held 70% of the total wealth in American households and owned four-fifths of all money in financial institutions.[13] While the GFC has made a dent in this group's retirement savings, Boomers remain a commercial and economic force not to be underestimated.

Looking overseas, startling recent figures out of the UK highlight the levels of financial prosperity among the Boomer generation. According to the British National Institute of Economic and Social Research the over-50s now have £8 out of every £10 and are, by far, the biggest owners and traders of shares.[14]

3 STYLISH

Brands are of critical importance to Boomers. This generation connects with advertising that focuses on how a product enhances the consumer's image and status rather than simply servicing a need.

Interestingly, Boomers were the first generation to put clothing labels on the *outside* of clothes... and they've stayed there ever since!

4 ASSERTIVE

The Boomers' demographic size has afforded them a weight and influence like no other generation before them. Whether in a consumer market or in politics, Boomers have always tended to get what they want because business, like politics, is a numbers game and this generation have the numbers on their side.

A perfect example of this can be seen in their drive for exceptional customer service. This has come as a direct result of the Boomers' demand for greater efficiency and excellence in what they buy.

5 AFRAID OF AGING

When it comes to aging, the Boomers have worked hard to move the goal posts further and further along the age scale. To be 'old' may have once meant being in your 60s. Now, they are calling that 'middle-aged'. Even the labels have changed. 'Mature-aged workers' are those who were previously called 'veterans'.

"BOOMERS WERE THE FIRST GENERATION TO PUT CLOTHING LABELS ON THE *OUTSIDE* OF CLOTHES."

The race against time is one that Boomers are desperate to win no matter how great the pain or expense. From Botox to laser lifts, being youthful is a top priority. The leading ladies of the hit show Desperate Housewives embody the confidence, beauty, youthfulness and independence that many Boomer women aspire to.

While face lifts and breast augmentations are nothing new, data released by the American Association of Anti-Aging Medicine in

2006 boasted industry-wide earnings of over $56 billion in the US alone! Even more staggering is the prediction that this turnover was expected to reach almost $80 billion over the next 3 years. These figures are a clear indication of the desire among Baby Boomer women (and increasingly, men) to spare no expense in their quest to feel younger and live longer.[15]

As a humorous reflection on this point, the then 23-year-old author Grainger David wrote in Fortune magazine of his parents' generation:

It looks as though you're trying to become the first fully reconstructed generation in history... complete with bionic knees, implanted hearing aids, regenerated hair, negative cholesterol and vacuum-cleaned colons.[16]

Baby Boomers are looking set to live out their days in the style and comfort to which they have become accustomed. Far from hoping to have accumulated enough to leave something for the kids, Boomers joke that retirement is one big exercise in spending their kid's inheritance. They have redefined the whole concept of old age and retirement. This, like every other stage of life that the Boomers have been through, will look very different when they are finished with it.

5 CHAPTER FIVE
GENERATION X

It would be fair to say that our next group, Generation X, grew up largely in the shadow of the Boomers. Born between the mid-1960s and early 1980s, Xers are a significantly smaller generation numerically than the Boomers and had the misfortune of entering the world just as the vibrant 1960s gave way to the more sedate and less prosperous 1970s.

The labels this generation have been given throughout their lives give us an indication of their reputation. From the *lost generation* to the *hopeless generation*, Xers have suffered under the burden of some less than flattering titles.

In stark contrast to the bright, jubilant and prosperous post-war era that the Boomers knew growing up, the Xers entered a society that was rapidly losing its luster and fraying around the edges.

Controversial bestselling author and Gen Xer, Bret Easton Ellis, described this sentiment in the *New York Times* in December 1990:

Few of my generation were alive, much less remember, the assassination of John F Kennedy. However, the oldest of us, even at the age of two, could sense something had gone wrong. For the rest of our childhood, things seemed to go that way...[17]

In the same vein, social researcher Mark McCrindle quotes a focus group participant who described being a Gen Xer as 'like arriving at the party a few hours late – there is a sense that it was once buzzing, but all that remains are a few cold sausage rolls and some flat punch.'[18]

Generation X was born into a new era and raised in a different way. As a reaction to the often overbearing control that the Xer's parents experienced in their own childhood, this new generation was given a level of freedom that, in hindsight, perhaps bordered on neglect. Xers were expected to grow up quickly, and subsequently developed a street-wise nature that is still very much a part of their psyche. Writing of this generation as teenagers, child psychologist David Elkind said:

Teenagers are expected to confront life and its challenges with a maturity once expected only of the middle-aged... High schools, which were once the setting for a unique teenage culture and language, have become miniatures of the adult community. Theft, violence, sex and substance abuse are now as common in high schools as they are on the streets.[19]

While the degree to which this description applies can depend on the region, school or other socio-economic factors, Generation X certainly experienced a childhood void of the innocence that previous generations had enjoyed. In just 20 years the highest rating television show among teenagers went from being *The Brady Bunch* to *Degrassi Junior High*.

Graeme Codrington describes how, for the first time, newspapers talked about the violence, not in a distant country, but down the street. Mass-murders, sexual abuse and police brutality changed the way an entire generation felt about the world around them. Society began to lock everything twice and hold its handbags and wallets a little tighter.[20]

At home, Xers encountered many other changes that profoundly shaped their views on family, relationships and identity. Between 1940 and 1980, divorce rates increased by over 300%[21] to the point where almost half of all marriages ended in divorce. For previous generations home was the place where a child could find security, stability and support. Far from the days of *Father Knows Best*, just having a father at home became, for many, a fantasy belonging to a bygone era.

Family relationships became more complicated: *'Mom's previous ex-husband', 'my stepsister's father's ex-wife', 'Dad's new boyfriend'*.[22] One Xer I know experienced her parents' divorce at a young age and had her father re-marry twice. As a result she has a half-brother and half-sister she lived with for six years but has not seen for seven, since the break-up of that family. As she describes it, her family structure looks less like a tree and more like a vineyard!

Even in cases where both parents maintained a stable relationship Xers saw another significant shift in the home dynamic – that of the double income family.

Mothers entered the workforce in droves leaving this generation with yet another label – *Latchkey Kids* – reflecting the fact that so many children came home from school to find empty houses. They would then have to let themselves in and wait for mom or dad to get home from work.

Adding to the confusion and upheaval that marked an Xer's childhood was the constant threat of nuclear war and the AIDS virus.

Named on 27 July 1982, Acquired Immune Deficiency Syndrome, or AIDS, was the new disease to strike fear into a generation of young people who were just coming of age. *How did you get it? Was there a cure? Where did it come from?* A great deal of myth and hysteria surrounded AIDS throughout the 1980s and into the early 1990s.

Interestingly, one of the greatest challenges facing health educators today is to get Generation Y to worry about AIDS at all! After all, to this younger generation AIDS is something that happens 'over there' in the developing world. It is not

"BETWEEN 1940 AND 1980, DIVORCE RATES INCREASED BY OVER 300%."

a perceived threat. This dangerous complacency is largely due to the fact that Gen Ys didn't grow up around the propaganda and scaremongering that instilled fear in their predecessors, the Xers.

Gen X feared nuclear war in much the same way. Following a session I delivered to a group of teachers in late 2006, I spoke with one Xer who described her experience growing up in the early 1970s. Speaking of her generation's fear of nuclear warfare, she told me that each New Year's Eve she remembered wondering if this would be the year when the world would end in a nuclear holocaust. I would suggest that Generation Y have no conscious fear of such an occurrence… it is simply not the perceived danger that it was for their older cousins, the Xers.

A product of their times, Generation X were often dismissed by older generations as rebellious youngsters who were disenchanted with the world. Many of their prevailing characteristics, however, have stayed with them into adulthood and don't look like changing any time soon.

CHARACTERISTICS OF GENERATION X

1 SKEPTICAL

Once bitten twice shy, Xers aren't swayed by the spin that can so easily convince their parents but instead they take everything with a grain of salt.

Graeme Codrington argues that the institution of government – be it through scandals (Watergate), half-truths (the Iraq War) or personal failures (Clinton and Lewinsky) – has demonstrated to Gen X that it cannot be trusted. Likewise, big business and global multi-nationals have been shown to be corrupt, unreliable and unethical. [23]

It's no wonder then, that 'smaller is better' is a motto which reflects and resonates with the Gen X mind-set. They are suspicious of working for and, hence, aligning themselves with organizations that seem to be big machines within which they can only ever be a small cog. Xers prefer to work in team-based relationship-driven environments.

2 CYNICAL

As they graduated from school and university in the late 80s, Xers boldly approached a corporate world which neither wanted nor needed them. Even today, the dominance of Boomers in the workforce means that many Gen Xers are still

"THE PERCEIVED UNWILLINGNESS OF BABY BOOMERS TO MOVE ON INTO RETIREMENT IS CREATING A GREAT SENSE OF RESENTMENT AND FRUSTRATION FOR XERS."

being prevented from rising to the positions they want, or deserve. The perceived unwillingness of Baby Boomers to move on into retirement is creating a great sense of resentment and frustration for Xers.

In his controversial book, *Please Just F* Off: It's Our Turn Now*, the wildly contentious author, Ryan Heath, outlines many of the 'beefs' that Gen X have with the Boomers.

His basic premise is that the Baby Boomers, due to their numerical size and clout as a generation, have robbed Gen X of the prosperity and opportunity they themselves have enjoyed. Validating this concern, it is actually predicted that Generation X will be the first American generation in history to earn less than their parents![24]

In the same vein, 41-year old American author Jeff Godinier suggests in his 2008 book X Saves the World that sandwiched between the Boomers and Gen Y, Generation X's limited demographic size will always condemn them to 'nicheville'. He goes on to bemoan the tyranny of the Boomers and their celebrity obsessed Gen Y offspring who 'suck up all the mass-media oxygen.'[25]

Whether the growing bitterness and resentment that Xers feel towards Boomers is reasonable or fair is largely irrelevant. The rift between these two groups is set to intensify as the clash of attitudes and mind-sets continues.

3 FLEXIBLE

Xers have come to learn one thing in life – *the only constant is change*. Fashions, fads and technology have changed with increasing frequency for this group.

Generation X has witnessed computers and cell phones evolving from luxury items to affordable necessities within their lifetime. The launch of the PC and the increased pace of communication and media has created a generation who are used to things being in a constant state of flux.

Among other things, this makes Generation X a highly valuable source of creativity and innovation in the workplace. They are constantly on the lookout for ways to change things. Even if it isn't broken, Xers will try and make it better or at least different to the way it was – just because they can. Whether it is moving the office furniture or tweaking the company motto, 'change for change's sake' is a philosophy Xers see as entirely acceptable and admirable. Boomers, however, tend to like preserving and protecting the more predictable status quo and so often find Gen Xers' love of change extremely frustrating.

> "'CHANGE FOR CHANGE'S SAKE' IS A PHILOSOPHY XERS SEE AS ENTIRELY ACCEPTABLE AND ADMIRABLE."

One downside to this characteristic is the ease with which this generation becomes bored. If things don't move at a pace that they find exciting they will be out the door and onto the next thing. Generation Xers are sure to get itchy feet if life stays the same for too long.

4 INDEPENDENT

Stemming from their days as Latchkey Kids, this generation has developed an independence and self-reliance that their parents and employers often find disconcerting.

As young people, many Xers sought independence in their early teen years. Feeling secure only when in control, they gained part-time work at the earliest possible age and couldn't move out of home fast enough. In stark contrast, Gen Ys are remaining dependant and living at home for as long as they possibly can. Much to the dismay of many parents, the current average age for Gen Y to move out of home of can be as high as 26 in some countries,[26] while in the US more than half of college graduates move back home after finishing fulltime study.[27]

Graeme Codrington suggests that Generation X's characteristics are perhaps best illustrated in their favorite cartoon character – Bart Simpson. As he describes it:

Bart is an irreverent, self-reliant free agent who is unconcerned with adults' opinions of him and is often the one to make allowances and amends for the many mistakes of his father. He is constantly challenging the rules 'just because he can' and although he is invariably in trouble, ultimately it all works out fine.[28]

5 NON-COLLECTIVIST

Unlike previous generations, Gen X lacked a common cause worth fighting for in their adolescent years. While the Builders united in the face of two World Wars and the Boomers had Vietnam, Xers have had no such rallying point.

As a result, Xers have fought battles for meaning, identity and purpose that tend to be more personalized and individual.

6 COMMITTED TO FRIENDS OVER FAMILY

Xers will often describe how, as children, they felt let down by the family unit – it did after all splinter just as they entered the world. Disappointed by the lack of family contact and nurturing in their childhood years, this generation's yearning for connection and belonging has led to a broadening of the definition of what constitutes 'family'.

A fascinating study in May 1998 in *USA Weekend* looked at who Gen Xers classified as 'family'. It found that family for this group was no longer about traditional concepts as much as the levels of emotional support found in a relationship. One interesting statistic cited in this article was that less than 20%

of this generation defined 'family' in terms of only the individuals to whom they are closely related by marriage or blood.

7 PRAGMATIC

Xers are far more interested in function than form. Like their younger cousins, Gen Y, they are not interested in whether something is right, correct and proper – they only care that something works. *Keep it real* is their motto.

6 CHAPTER SIX
GENERATION Y

As society saw Generation X move out of adolescence and into their early 20s, it became apparent that, for this generation, something had gone a little bit wrong. Teenage pregnancy was up, adolescent depression was widespread and youth suicide approached epidemic levels.

Unsure of what exactly had gone wrong with the Xers, the collective sentiment was that we as a society would do everything in our power to make sure that the next generation was different... very different.

Into this climate Generation Y was born. Almost overnight, society's mind-set towards raising children changed. Entering an era often dubbed 'The Decade of the Child', parents in the 1980s were asked, 'Have you hugged your child today?'

Cabbage Patch Dolls were the toy of choice. New child-friendly vans proudly displayed 'Baby on Board' signs. Generational gurus Strauss and Howe describe a parenting trend that moved away from neglect and negativism towards protection and support.[29]

In the early 1980s, the attitude towards the role and place of children shifted from 'children should be seen and not heard' to 'children are to be prized, protected and above all else pampered'. Teachers and employers frequently ask me why this younger generation think they are at the center of the universe. The simple answer to this question is that since birth they have been told, both implicitly and explicitly, that they *are*.

Generation Y were raised in the era of self esteem. From birth, this group were bombarded with the message that they were 'special', 'magnificent', 'unique', 'wonderful' and set to 'be a leader'. Professor Jean Twenge from San Diego State University

> "GENERATION Y CHILDREN AND TEENAGERS OFTEN HAVE WEEKLY SCHEDULES THAT ARE AS FULL AS THEIR CAREER-DRIVEN PARENTS."

notes that the number of psychology and education journal articles devoted to self esteem doubled between the 1970s and 1980s and increased a further 52% during the 1990s.[30]

In their formative years, Gen Y saw divorce rates and abortions begin to level off. Society began to place greater value on children and the emergence of 'spanking' as a social no-no was symbolic of a wider trend.

Being a working mother suddenly seemed less attractive. Rather than employment being a social statement indicating that you were an empowered, forward-thinking and ambitious woman, the new status symbol was the 'stay-at-home mom'.

In stark contrast to the Xers' experience of childhood, a *Newsweek* poll in May 2000 found that 61% of Gen Ys felt their parents spent enough time with them and 15% went as far as describing their parents as being around too much!

Gen Y's parents, the Boomers, have ensured that their children had every possible extracurricular opportunity afforded them. This has resulted in an increasing busy-ness in the lives of young people. Gen Y children and teenagers often have weekly schedules that are as full as their career-driven parents'. In a financial sense, no expense seems too great to guarantee that Gen Ys have the very best start in life.

Unsurprisingly, this generation exhibits a high self-esteem and confidence fostered by the constant encouragement they have received throughout their lives. They are very aware of their rights and are well informed when it comes to what they deserve in life – the best.

Although some dismiss Gen Y's self esteem as superficial and naive,[31] there is no doubt that it is all-pervasive. In one recent study of students aged 16-24, 82% believed that the next Bill Gates is in their generation, 51% said they know the next Bill Gates, and 24% said they believe they *are* the next Bill Gates.[32]

All that said, indications are that Generation Y are certainly living up to the hopes and dreams that society had for them following the Xers. They are well educated, ambitious, tolerant, tech-savvy and, perhaps surprisingly, socially aware.

Indicative of this positive trend are figures which show that 76% of 12th graders volunteered their time in 2001 compared with 64% in 1990.[33] Further still, in 2006, 69% of young people aged 13-25 considered a company's social and environmental commitment when deciding where to shop.[34] Gen Y are indeed a civic-minded generation with a conscience.

I recently spoke with the HR manager of a large insurance company about the increasing need for employers to be socially responsible. One interesting observation she made regarded the priority Gen Y place on wanting to work for organizations with a social conscience.

She recounted numerous instances of confident and articulate Gen Ys asking in the course of a job interview, 'Why should I work for you?' As American author Tim Elmore suggests, Gen Y desire their work to be transformational, not simply transactional.[35]

Further espousing the virtuous nature of this younger generation, *Newsweek* reporter Anna Quindlen writes:

The future will be grand because our kids will be its keepers... [Generation Y] *is more interesting, more confident, less uptight, better educated, more creative and in some essential fashion, unafraid. They are simply better than I was at their age and their peers are generous in ways unknown to me when I was young.*[36]

Well known author Don Tapscott cites further evidence of the positive trends being driven by Gen Y in his book *Grown Up Digital*. He points to a generalized reduction in the rates of teen suicide and violent crime along with lower alcohol and drug abuse amongst teens.[37]

Further still, there is early evidence that Gen Y are even showing a renewed commitment to family and more conservative values. In one 2007 poll, 90% of Gen Ys thought it was likely they would be married to the same person their whole life while 63% of Gen Y women reported that getting married and having children was more important to them than professional advancement.[38]

Interestingly, this picture is at odds with many popular stereotypes surrounding today's young people. As Don Tapscott so rightly suggests, the media are quick to tell us that Gen Y are a bunch of 'dull, celebrity-obsessed, net-addicted, shopaholic exhibitionists with a taste for violence, online and offline'.[39] Many of the teachers, parents and employers I speak to also describe Generation Y in terms that are anything but flattering. They speak of a generation that is disrespectful, self-centered, disloyal, unfocused and arrogant.

So which picture is more accurate?

In answering this question, I would argue that Gen Y are no better or worse than previous generations and that rating generations using such terms is both inappropriate and unhelpful. Generation Y are simply different. They come from a different era and are a product of the time into which they were born. Their mind-set, world view and approach differ from that of older generations in a number of significant ways.

Section two will focus on these differences as we take an in-depth look at how Gen Y's paradigm differs from that of their parents, teachers and employers.

However, before we look at the final generation of the 20th century, Generation Z, let's summarize what we have covered so far. US generational expert Eric Chester provides a good snapshot of how much has changed in recent decades:[40]

TOPIC	BOOMERS	XERS	GEN Y
TELEVISION	*Bonanza*	*Family Ties*	*Jerry Springer*
WEALTH	I'll earn it	I don't care that much about it	Gimme, or I'll take it.
ROLE MODELS	Men of character	Men and *women* of character	What's character?
EMPLOYMENT ATTITUDES	Jobs are hard to find.	I'll work if I have to.	Jobs are a dime a dozen.
LOYALTY TO EMPLOYER	I'll work my way to the top.	This could lead to the top.	If I can't take Saturday off, I'll quit.
JUSTICE	Always prevails	Usually prevails.	Can be bought.
EDUCATION	Tell me *what* to do.	Show me *how* to do it.	Show me *why* to do it.
RESPECTING ELDERS	Is automatic	Is polite.	Is earned not assumed.
PERSONAL DEBT	Only if I have to.	If I really want something.	How much can I get?
ROCK STARS	Little Richard, Elvis, Alice Cooper	Boy George, Ozzy Osbourne, Madonna	Marilyn Manson, Nirvana, Eminem
CHANGE	Dislike	Accept	Demand
TECHNOLOGY	Ignorant of	Comfortable with	Masters of
VIDEO GAMES	*Pong*	*PacMan*	*Mortal Kombat*
PORNOGRAPHY	In movie theatres	In video stores	In TV ads
COMMUNICATION	Via parents' phone	Via personal phone	Cell phone, email, chat rooms

7 CHAPTER SEVEN
GENERATION Z

The final generation to be born into the 20th century, Generation Z, are the children currently filling our kindergartens, elememtary schools and day care centers. Even though Gen Z are still too young to profile with any great certainty, the early signs indicate that this is a group who are:

1 TECH SAVVY

Gen Zs have only known a world where instant connectivity is the norm – a generation who in their short lives have had unprecedented access to and understanding of technology and instant gratification. Consider the fact that most Gen Zs have never seen a camera that requires film much less had to wait for photos to be developed!

Gen Z's exposure to technology is starting early with one recent study indicating that almost two thirds of babies under the age of one are spending an average of one hour and twenty minutes in front of a TV or computer screen each day.[41] Many toddlers know their way around an iPhone by age 2 and even have apps on a parent's device that have been downloaded specifically for them to play with.

Resulting from this trend, childhood has become a largely indoor experience for the Zs. For much of this generation only a small fraction of free time is spent playing outdoors. Entertainment, play and social interaction increasingly revolve around televisions, computers and video games with Gen Z currently dedicating 27% of their waking hours to screen time.[42] As a worrying confirmation of this trend, Richard Louv in his book *Last Child in the Woods* points to a 50% decline in recent years of children aged nine to twelve spending time in outdoor activities (hiking, walking, fishing, beach play).[43]

During a recent vacation on a resort island near Australia's Great Barrier Reef, my wife and I were intrigued to witness the complex technological and social habits of Gen Z first-hand. Throughout the week of our stay we noticed three young girls from the same family who spent most of their time playing each other wirelessly on their Nintendo DSs. From the second we all boarded the 12-seater plane out to the island to the moment we arrived back on the mainland seven days later, these girls seemed to do little else than have their eyes glued to the game console screens. I found myself doing what so many older generations do – making judgements about how these girls spent their time in comparison to what I did at the same age. I caught myself condemning the fact that these young girls chose to play computer games rather than enjoying the scenery, riding the jet skis and going on real-life adventures in the rainforest. However, I recognized the need to stop and remember that these girls are simply a result of the world they have known. Their choice of how they have fun isn't any worse than mine – it is just different. Furthermore, I recognized that they have highly developed technical skills in communication, networking and problem solving that I can't even imagine. What's more, these skills are ones they are developing while they play, not through any formal training or conscious effort.

Highlighting this trend, a recent study conducted by market research firm *Knowledge Networks/SRI* revealed that 61% of Gen Zs have televisions in their rooms, 35% have video games and 14% have a DVD player. Of those who have a television in their room 75% report multitasking with other media while watching TV.[44]

Mark McCrindle describes the Zs as a generation 'who have only known a wireless, hyperlinked, user-generated world where they are only ever a few clicks away from any piece of knowledge.'[45]

While such access to information may be a very positive thing, a British report that was cited in The Daily Telegraph in March 2008 found that a frighteningly large number of under-16-year-olds spend more than 20 hours per week on the internet. Worryingly, they also found that 57% of children have seen online pornography, most of it accidentally in the form of pop-up ads.

Much of this exposure to technology and media from a young age leads on to the second characteristic researchers are witnessing in Generation Z – a lowering of the age of innocence and a premature maturity.

2 PREMATURELY MATURE

Zs are exposed to more, experience more, and experiment more at a younger age, than previous generations. Added to the societal influences shaping this, physiological and environmental factors also have a role to play. Today, puberty hits boys and girls one to two years earlier than it did thirty years ago.[46]

Physiology aside, popular culture and media saturation are undoubtedly the key causal factors in a lowering of the age of innocence in Gen Z. As sociology professor Tony Campolo puts it, we have a generation of children who "know too much too soon."[47] This young group are the most marketed-to generation of children the world has ever seen and it is estimated they are exposed to between 30,000-40,000 TV commercials each year.[48]

Of great concern is the fact that body image is becoming an issue of increasing concern for both boys and girls in early *primary school* rather than early high school. Parenting expert Michael Grose points to startling research by author and beauty stylist Gregory Landsman which found that children as young as six reportedly disliked their bodies and found themselves unattractive.[49]

Leading Australian demographer Hugh Mackay highlighted Gen Z's premature maturity in an editorial he wrote for The Sydney Morning Herald on 12 January, 2008. Speaking of the fact that children's parties are becoming quasi-adolescent affairs, he described the growth of the Adolescent Childhood (AC) syndrome. This syndrome is one that Mackay suggests is reflected in the curious desire of parents to hasten their children's development toward adulthood by encouraging them to act like mini-adults. Looking at how this trend relates directly to raising girls, Mackay argues that the machinery of modern marketing has encouraged parents to buy their daughters clothes, shoes, cosmetics, dolls and music designed to 'create the illusion of a precocious, premature sexuality'.[50]

While we are only seeing early signs of the impact of this trend on childhood development, it will be interesting to see how Gen Z approaches adolescence when so much of the sense of discovery, innocence and curiosity associated with this stage of life in past eras has been lost.

3 PAMPERED

Gen Z are growing up with fewer siblings than children of previous generations. Census data indicates that around 60% of families with Gen Z children have two kids or less and currently the average family has just 3.2 members including the parents.[51]

As a result of shrinking family sizes, attention, affection and money are being lavished on this young generation like none before. There are early indications of a self-centered individualism among Gen Z that eclipses anything we have seen in Gen Y.

It should be no great surprise when concepts such as compromise, team playing and sharing are seen as foreign to Gen Z. After all, many of them have been treated like mom or dad's little prince or princess since birth.

4 EMPOWERED

While empowerment is typically a very positive thing, the way in which Gen Z are being empowered from a very young age is resulting in some unintended and challenging consequences.

No longer are they simply toddlers or children – young Gen Zs are called 'little people'. It is almost as if children are now simply seen as miniature versions of adults. As such, they are expected to have the same level of discernment, self-control and capacity for reasoning that was previously not expected until an individual's late teens or early twenties.

Prof. Jean Twenge picks up on this trend in her book *Generation Me.* Highlighting how parents begin asking children their preferences even before the child can answer, Prof. Twenge contrasts modern parenting approaches with those adopted in past eras. She points to the trend of parents who would never dream of making every single decision for their child without first asking what the child wants – a far cry from the 'be seen and not heard' days where children fitted in around the parent's lives and not vice versa. Twenge argues that this results in children coming to believe that their wants are the most important."[52]

To look at how this empowerment plays out in everyday life, consider the example of a mother instructing her three year old daughter to clean up her toys and place them back in the box at the end of playtime. Twenty years ago, the mother may have instructed her daughter to do so with the warning that failure to comply would result in a spanking. Today however with spanking such a societal taboo, the pressure on mom now is to ask her daughter how she would *feel* about putting her toys back in the box and then outlining 20 alternative courses of action from which the child is to choose the one that suits her best!

Indeed, Gen Z are being raised in an era where they have more power and more choices than children in previous generations did. It waits to be seen how this will impact on their approach to notions of responsibility, deference and submission as they move into adolescence and beyond.

5 RISK AVERSE

For older generations risk is seen as directly related to return – nothing ventured, nothing gained. Builders and Boomers were taught to manage risk, 'hedge their bets' and 'go out on a limb' in order to achieve and grow.

The adventurous, inquisitive and pioneering spirit of previous generations has paved the way for many of the inventions and discoveries that we now take for granted. Throwing caution to the wind and overcoming a seemingly insurmountable challenge had an attraction for older generations.

Builders and Boomers grew up in a time when cots were painted with lead-based paint and nobody knew any better. Children stayed out playing all day completely out of contact with their parents and knew when it was time to head home because the street lights came on.

Accidents were simply that. No-one was to blame and they were just a part of life. If you fell over in the street you actually hoped no-one saw it – having witnesses was the last thing you wanted! There was never any question of who was responsible for taking risks – naturally it was the individual taking them.

In contrast, Generation Z has grown up in an era where risk has become unacceptable and 'throwing caution to the wind' is akin to negligence.

These days, risk seems too frightening a proposition for many young people. After all, it could lead to failure, danger, disappointment and harm. Fear is a powerful driving force in our modern age – fear of failure, fear of the unknown, fear of terrorists, fear of neighbors – but, most of all, fear of being sued.

Regrettably, we live in a litigious world where accidents are no longer just accidents. Someone is always to blame – and it can't be me!

Rather than being seen as a necessary part of living in the real world, risk has become public enemy number one.

In a recent article in *The Daily Telegraph*, Sydney University Health Sciences Professor, Anita Bundy, argued that safety-first measures have all but killed off the fun of today's playgrounds. She said:

You need things where kids can be safe but where there is a bit of perceived risk – they shouldn't be able to fall on their head easily, but it can't be so safe that they are bored to tears.[53]

With such a focus on shielding Gen Z from risk, it is reasonable to wonder how this will affect their approach to innovation, adventure and entrepreneurialism as they grow older. Furthermore, how will this group's personal development and sense of identity be shaped by a world where they never have to experience risk, pain, disappointment or failure? After all, we learn best by challenging physical boundaries, taking risks and experiencing a certain degree of pain. As author and columnist Lenore Skenazy so rightly attests, kids who aren't allowed to take any risks turn out to be less safe than those who do![54]

Gen Z's aversion to academic risk is also highlighted by elementary school teachers who often talk of the reluctance among this generation to raise their hand in class to answer questions. Whereas Gen Y tended to exhibit a bold self-assurance and confidence in their younger years, Gen Z seem acutely afraid of being wrong – failure, it seems, is not an option for this group.

6 PROTECTED

While it may be nothing new for older generations to wax lyrical that "today's kids have it too easy", there is a strong and growing sense of worry amongst many grandparents that their Gen Z grandchildren are being raised as 'cotton wool kids'. This sentiment seems to extend into the general community as well with almost two thirds of respondents in a recent parenting survey indicating that they believe today's kids are over-protected.[55]

Indeed, Gen Z are being raised in an environment where they are being guarded and protected by their largely Gen X parents. Ironically, whereas Gen X were raised with unprecedented levels of freedom, they themselves are the infamous 'helicopter parents.'

While the parents of Gen Z may be very fearful for the safety of their children, the data indicates that such anxiety is largely unfounded. Despite the fact that 80% of parents report being afraid for their children's safety (particularly outdoors or in public)[56] current rates of violent crime against young people have actually fallen to below 1975 levels.[57]

On top of going to great lengths to protect their children's safety, wellbeing and self esteem, there is a growing trend amongst the parents of Gen Z to shield children from the consequences, negative emotions and the realities of life.

This is perhaps most clearly seen in the behaviour of over-zealous parents who come to the rescue and defense of children at the first hint of disciplinary measures being taken at school. I have heard countless stories from teachers of students messaging parents when their teacher sends them from the room, removes a privilege or dares to give a detention. Before the end of the lesson, parents have arrived at the

> "GENERATION Z HAS GROWN UP IN AN ERA WHERE RISK HAS BECOME UNACCEPTABLE AND 'THROWING CAUTION TO THE WIND' IS AKIN TO NEGLIGENCE."

school ready for a fight: *'It couldn't be my son; my daughter would never do that; you must have been mistaken'* and the list goes on. Is it any wonder that teachers recently rated dealing with parents as their number one professional headache.[58]

Indicative of how out of control this parental compulsion to shield children from consequences is becoming, one principal recently reported two separate instances in the past year of parents arriving at school accompanied by the family lawyer in order to defend their child against disciplinary measures taken by the teacher. While it is tempting to dismiss such cases as unique and exceptional, one recent survey found that 20% of school principals spend five to ten hours per week writing reports or having meetings simply in order to avoid litigation.[59]

In addition to shielding their children from consequences, many Gen X parents also feel compelled to protect their Gen Z children from negative emotions in life too. This is evidenced by the modern version of the childhood party game 'pass the parcel' where every child now gets a prize to prevent disappointment. Then there are the parents who purchase in-car DVD players so their children don't experience the dull ache of boredom during car trips.

While protection and nurture are perfectly natural parental instincts, there is a real possibility that Gen Z are being shielded from the consequences of their actions and the realities of life to the detriment of their character development and resiliency.

Perhaps we need to work toward a better balance between letting our children experience the negative aspects of life and overprotecting them. To this end, I think American politician Ivy Baker Priest offers a healthy perspective on parenting:

My father had always said that there are four things a child needs – plenty of love, nourishing food, regular sleep, and lots of soap and water – and after those, what they need most is some intelligent neglect.

Despite some of the more concerning trends emerging in Gen Z, there is certainly a lot to be excited about with this group too! Early signs are that Gen Z are an incredibly switched on group of youngsters who are technologically adept, environmentally aware and supremely confident.

It bears repeating that Gen Z is probably still too young to profile or describe in a definitive way. However, the characteristics of this new generation will undoubtedly be marked by the unique societal climate of their upbringing.

Recently watching an elderly Builder interacting with his Gen Z great-grandchild highlighted for me just how dramatically things have changed in one century. If you thought Gen Y were different, wait till Generation Z start making their presence felt!

WHY CAN'T EVERYONE ELSE JUST BE NORMAL... LIKE ME?

2

At this point, you may well be wondering why I have spent so much time looking at each of these different generational groups. You may well be asking why it is important to understand Baby Boomers in a book which is meant to be about understanding Generation Y.

As I indicated in the introductory pages, the reason why understanding your generational background is so critical comes down to one thing… your paradigm.

Why can't everyone else just be normal… like me?

When I first read this sentence in Graeme Codrington's book *Mind the Gap,* I realized that it indeed captures the essence of all conflict and friction between generations. After all, the way we dress, the music we enjoy, the TV shows we like and the careers we value seem perfectly *normal* to us. So if *we* are normal, what's wrong with everyone else?

> "PARADIGMS ARE THE JUDGEMENTS THAT WE PLACE ON OUR PERCEPTIONS OF THE PEOPLE AND WORLD AROUND US."

We each tend to approach other generations with the underpinning mind-set that our view of the world is the most considered, well-informed and reasonable view. Naturally, anyone whose paradigm differs from our own is in need of convincing, correcting or perhaps even punishing.

Paradigms are defined as *'the set of assumptions, concepts, values, and practices that constitute a way of viewing reality'*. Put more simply, paradigms are the judgements that we place on our perceptions of the people and world around us.

More than you know, your paradigm of what is correct, fair, appropriate, good and bad has been powerfully shaped by, among other things, the era of your birth. Of course, this is inconsequential when dealing with and relating to your contemporaries – they are, after all, quite likely to agree with and affirm your perceptions and judgements.

However, what happens when perceptions differ?

What happens when paradigms clash?

I recently received an email which perfectly illustrated the conflict caused when opposing paradigms clash. The email contained a transcript of a radio conversation between a US Naval ship and the Canadian authorities off the coast of Newfoundland in October 1995. It read:

US Ship: *Please divert your course 0.5 of a degree to the south to avoid a collision.*

Coastguard: *We recommend you divert your course 15 degrees to the south to avoid a collision.*

US Ship: *This is the Captain of a US Navy ship. I say again, divert YOUR course.*

Coastguard: *No. I say again, you divert YOUR course!*

US Ship: *THIS IS THE AIRCRAFT CARRIER USS CORAL SEA. WE ARE A LARGE WARSHIP OF THE US NAVY. DIVERT YOUR COURSE NOW!*

Coastguard: *This is a lighthouse. It's your call.*

And with just that one sentence, everything changes. We call this a 'paradigm shift' – where we suddenly recognize that the way we are viewing the world is perhaps not the *only* way to view it!

Yet before we can make such a shift we must first acknowledge and appreciate the existence of 'paradigm *rifts*'. These rifts represent the gap that exists between how we perceive the world and how someone else perceives it. Such rifts can be caused by any

"CONTRARY TO POPULAR OPINION, GENERATION Y ARE NOT SIMPLY BABY BOOMERS WAITING TO GROW UP."

number of factors including race, religion and gender. However, one influence that is often overlooked is that of our generational background.

So prevalent are conflicts caused by the generation gap in the workplace that the majority of respondents in a recent global survey listed inter-generational conflicts as the greatest source of problems in the workplace above conflict caused by gender and culture gaps.[60]

While you could dismiss the differences you see in young people as merely 'a stage they are going through', the truth is that their paradigm, like your own, is a direct result of the era into which they were born. Like you, they won't just grow out of it. Contrary to popular opinion, Generation Y are not simply Baby Boomers waiting to grow up.

The challenge is to recognize *how* and *why* Generation Y are different. In this section, I will highlight nine areas of paradigm rift and compare a traditional or established generational mind-set (shared by Builders, Boomers and the leading edge of Gen X) with that of Generation Y. I have chosen to focus on these nine areas as they are the ones that cause the most friction and conflict between Gen Ys and their teachers, parents and employers.

When I discuss the concept of paradigm rift in my presentations on *Engaging Generation Y*, I tend to illustrate the two different mind-sets by using two sets of glasses – those of an older person and those that would generally be worn by a Gen Y. These two pairs of glasses are a metaphor for the lenses through which we view the world. I like to use this illustrative tool because glasses and the lenses they contain are very similar to paradigms in that both shape the perceptions and judgements that an individual makes without changing the inherent nature of what is being viewed. Depending on the paradigm lens you are looking through, the world can look very different as you will quickly see.

8 CHAPTER EIGHT
NINE AREAS OF
PARADIGM RIFT

1 CONCEPT OF TRUTH

Established Generational Lens

Through an established generational lens truth is absolute. There is black and there is white. There is right and there is wrong. I learn what is right and what is wrong by listening to those with either the moral or academic authority to teach me. According to one recent survey, 70% of Builders and almost two-thirds of Boomers agreed that there are such things as moral absolutes.[61]

This 'black and white' way of looking at truth is called a 'modernist mind-set'. For modernists, the pursuit of truth is linked strongly to morality. Modernists are interested in hearing others' versions of truth so they can more adequately determine the line between right and wrong.

The motto of a school I spoke at recently best depicted a modernist mind-set; *Truth through knowledge*.

Modernists want to be persuaded and convinced. They will insist on seeing the statistics, data, research and empirical evidence that give weight and credibility to the truth being taught.

For a modernist the key question in learning is, 'Why should I listen to what you are saying?' Authorial intent and the credibility of the individual imparting the information and truth is vital.

Modernists place great emphasis on the outward symbols of credibility – the letters after your name, where your office is in the building or the color of the robes you wear if in public office.

In conversation you can often tell quite quickly if the person you are speaking with is a modernist because they will say one word with remarkable predictability and frequency – *should*. This is a powerful word as it places a judgement on something that was previously neutral. In other

> "FOR THE POSTMODERNIST, THE VERY SUGGESTION THAT YOUR VERSION OF TRUTH IS MORE VALID THAN THEIRS IS DISMISSED AS NAIVETY OR ARROGANCE."

words, a modernist will be quick to tell you how you *should* think, what you *should* believe, what you *should* say, how you *should* act.

To a modernist, 'should' is an entirely appropriate word to use when prescribing the response or actions of another. After all, if something is self-evidently correct and proper, then to hold an opinion or have a perception otherwise must be incorrect, misinformed or just plain wrong.

Of course, the challenge arises when this paradigm comes into contact with a generation for whom the word 'should' simply does not resonate.

Generation Y Lens

For Generation Y, truth is not absolute, rather truth is *relative*. This group tends to adopt a mind-set towards truth that is most commonly called 'postmodern'. If I look at truth through a *postmodern* Gen Y lens, I recognize that what's true for me is a result of my background, my experiences, my story and how I have perceived the world. More significantly though, I understand that *your* version of truth is a result of your background, experiences and perceptions.

If your version of truth is completely opposite to mine, and our world views are diametrically opposed, a modernist would insist (if they were not too politically correct to do so) that one of us must be right and one of us must be wrong. The goal then would be to figure out who is right and who is wrong. Logic may be employed, statistics may be quoted, persuasive tactics may be used and a full-blown argument may ensue. However, in the end, at least one of us will be absolutely certain who is right.

For the postmodernist, however, the key distinction is that both versions of truth, even though they are at odds with each other, are equally *valid*. In other words, a postmodernist is comfortable with accepting differences in world views without feeling the need to prove themselves as more credible, experienced or informed than someone with a different take on reality.

While such a world view is often celebrated as a very positive step toward an increased acceptance of diversity, the challenging implications of a postmodern perspective are many and varied. Professor Jean Twenge from San Diego State University cites numerous cases of lecturers returning essays to students with corrected spelling mistakes or answers marked as wrong only to be met with the student response of 'well that's just your opinion'.[62]

For the postmodernist, the very suggestion that your version of truth is more valid than theirs – or even worse, that they are wrong – is dismissed as naivety or arrogance. The word 'should' therefore holds little or no relevance. The moment you start 'should-ing' Generation Y, what is the first question they ask? That's right... *why?*

Many members of older generations see this 'why?' as a belligerent, rhetorical question designed to challenge their authority. That is, however, not necessarily the case. Rather, it expresses a desire to understand the perceptions that have led you to make the judgements that you have. Can I suggest to older generations that the way you respond to the question of 'why?' is critical to the level of engagement you will have with Gen Y. If you automatically dismiss the question ('because I said so') or respond with a patronizing put-down, engagement will be the furthest thing from your reality with this group.

Contrary to popular opinion, Gen Y *is* interested in hearing your version of truth. They will not automatically dismiss your ideas, insights and opinions simply because they are different from their own. They are not, however, looking to be persuaded by your logic or evidence. They want to hear your version of truth, not so they can learn what is black and white, but rather to expand their shades of gray. Recognizing the challenges that exist in connecting with such a world view, American authors Rick and Kathy Hicks, offer some valuable insights for parents looking to communicate with their postmodern children:

A Plea for Acceptance

Just because I am different to you, please don't reject me or discount my worth. Don't assume I am wrong and try to change me.

If I see things differently than you do, please try to consider why (or even ask me) what was different about the world I grew up in than the one you experienced?

If my passions are stronger – or weaker – than yours, take time to discover the reason why rather than judging me as radical, immoral, lazy, or indifferent. Please don't assume that, because we have different values, one of us has to be wrong. Be open to the possibility that many issues are more a matter of preference than morality.

Try not to take it personally when I don't see or do things the way that you would. Please realize that my values are deeply ingrained from my past (as are yours) and my actions aren't necessarily a rejection of your values but an expression of mine.

When you accept me in spite of our differences, you are telling me that I am worthy of your respect, friendship and love. Your acceptance tells me that our relationship doesn't depend on me always agreeing with you or being just like you. I can be free to be me and you can be free to be you.

We may have to agree to disagree on certain issues but disagreeing doesn't mean we value each other less.

As I feel secure in your unconditional acceptance of me, I'll have the freedom to listen to you without being defensive. You can help me understand why you believe the way you do and who knows… I just may be able to see your point of view and even come to the discovery that you just might be right – but that choice has to be mine.[63]

That said, a postmodern approach to truth does create a number of issues at a societal level. For example, if there really are no absolutes, rules or fixed notions of right and wrong, where do the concepts of justice, morality and personal responsibility come in?

In his poem *Family Business,* Australian poet Stephen Davis describes some of the limitations and challenges of a postmodern mind-set in its purest form:

If there never is a moral standard,
if nothing's ever really right or wrong,
then throw out your old grandma and grandad
and sell your spouse and children for a song.

Steal your neighbor's car and smash their windows,
kick their moggy hard and stomp their roses,
set fire to their house next time the wind blows:
it's your perfect right then, I suppose
no one can tell you what you've done is bad.

Relativity is open-minded,
never judges someone sane or mad,
has no benchmarks, so it's never blinded
by someone else's pain or point of view.
Did I hurt you, love? Tough. What's wrong with you?

Reconciling the differences between a modernist and postmodernist world view is set to be a flashpoint for conflict and tension in the coming years. It is no longer enough to fall back on the assumptions and foundations of morality and truth that society has always taken for granted.

Evidence of Gen Y's increasingly fluid perspective on truth and morality is found in research which shows that 74% of today's high school students admit to cheating in assessments compared with 61% in 1992. In addition more than a quarter of high school boys admitted having shoplifted from a store at least once.[64]

Picking up on this trend, social researcher Mark McCrindle points to the emerging "it's only a crime if you get caught" attitude prevalent in many young people today. He goes on to suggest that in an era where truth is relative and context, interpretation and individual circumstances dominate, upholding laws and regulations is an increasing challenge.[65]

Everything is going to be questioned and tested by the next generation. Nothing, it seems, is sacred. How older generations react to this will be the biggest determining factor in achieving a level of engagement with Gen Y. Communicating truth and responding to the 'why' question represents a great challenge but also a tremendous opportunity for older generations. This is something I will look at more in section three.

2 RESPECT

Established Generational Lens

To the established generations, respect is an honor *bestowed* on a person, position or institution that deserves respect.

Growing up, older generations were instructed to respect their elders. In other words, they were told to 'respect that person simply because they have been breathing for longer than you!'

Respect, this group was taught, was to be shown to those in positions of authority. From the schoolteacher to the police officer and the local parish priest, respect was to be given on the basis of role.

These days, things have certainly changed.

When speaking to audiences about the notion of respect across different generations, I often like to do a quick survey. I particularly like to ask teachers how many of them feel there has been at least one occasion in the previous week when respect was not automatically shown to them simply because they were standing at the front of the classroom. This question is always greeted with laughter and a unanimous show of hands.

Why is this? The answer, in part, is because Gen Y's approach to respect is very different to that of previous generations.

Generation Y Lens

One of the most common complaints you will hear against Gen Y is that they are disrespectful. The media tends to highlight stories that reinforce this stereotype. Whether it is students who won't give up their seat on the bus or delinquents vandalising war memorials, Gen Y are often cited as a self-centered group who exhibit a chronic lack of respect for everyone and everything.

> "GENERATION Y WILL GIVE RESPECT - IT IS JUST THAT THE PATHWAY THERE IS QUITE DIFFERENT."

My experience with this generation, however, has left me convinced that Generation Y *will* give respect – it is just that the pathway there is quite different. To Gen Y, respect is not bestowed – it must be *earned*.

They would tell you that being worthy of respect is like being a nice person; if you have to repeatedly claim that you are (and then enforce the point), then perhaps you really aren't.

Rather than something they lack, respect is in fact a core value for Gen Ys. Respect is the currency of their relationships. You may have heard them say: *'Don't dis' me'*. When translated, this statement actually means: *'Don't disrespect me'*.

Generation Y will show respect but under two key conditions:

A) Reciprocity

If you want respect from Generation Y start by showing it to them. Respect must be a two-way deal.

One local council in Sydney truly understands this point. Walking around the popular beachside suburb of Manly you will see signs outlining behaviors which are socially unacceptable. These signs list rules like *do not litter*, *don't throw things at passing cars* and *do not urinate in public*.

While most local councils have similar signage in public places, Manly Council is doing something subtly but powerfully different. At the bottom of their signs, once they've outlined all their do's and don'ts, they have one key sentence which reads: *We respect you, you respect us.*

This one sentence speaks volumes to Generation Y. The council is not merely outlining a list of shoulds to be complied with. Rather, they are in essence saying: *We respect your rights as a young person who wants to have a good time. However, we ask for your respect in return. Here is the list of ways by which you can show that respect.* See the difference in this approach? Respect is now a conversation – it is reciprocal.

This is by no means a magic pill that will completely prevent anti-social and disrespectful behavior. It is, however, far more likely to connect with Gen Y than simply demanding respect for no other reason than that they *should* show it.

B) Relationship

Generation Y tends to show respect for relationships and individuals but not for roles and institutions. If they see you as a real person and feel a sense of rapport and connection with you as a teacher, parent or superior, you will find their respect is much easier to earn.

Hiding behind roles, titles and positions of power and control will only distance Gen Ys.

In section three I will touch on this point further with some ideas and strategies for building relationships and respect with this group.

3 PATIENCE

Established Generational Lens

To older generations patience is a virtue. Delayed gratification is the process of waiting for something and, in doing so, developing the character required to deal well with what you are waiting for. As such, the discomfort and frustration involved in exercising patience and delayed gratification are simply part of normal everyday existence and therefore not something to be avoided.

"GENERATION Y HAVE GROWN UP WITH FAST FOOD, PRE-PREPARED MEALS AND LIGHTNING-FAST INTERNET ACCESS."

Setbacks, frustrations and disappointments are par for the course. Persistence is the name of the game. Good things come to those who wait. Small beginnings are not to be despised and incremental growth is good enough.

The foundational belief that underpins an established generational approach to patience is that *life is meant to be hard.* While this was a lesson taught to older generations from the opposite perspective (life was never meant to be easy) the message was clear – when life gets hard, *that's life!* Challenges are not something to complain about or shy away from. Rather, they are a normal and expected part of daily living and they serve a purpose: they are there to grow and mature you.

Older generations tended to start their careers with the expectation that advancement would take time. Climbing the corporate ladder was not going to happen overnight. Career planning was spoken of in terms of years and sometimes decades. 'Paying your dues' was the pathway to progress and getting ahead often meant doing little more than waiting your turn.

Generation Y Lens

Through a Gen Y lens, however, patience is not a virtue. Rather, patience is pointless, frustrating and largely unacceptable.

If young people have to wait for something, rather than being seen as an indication that they are on the right track and should persist and stick at it, they see this as evidence that they must be waiting for the wrong thing and should swap to something that will happen faster and easier. For this group, good things don't come to those who wait – good things come to those who *make it happen*. This is the mind-set of the generation told by Nike to *Just Do It.*

If patience is a virtue, as older generations attest, do you suppose that an entire cohort of young people was somehow born inherently less virtuous, or is it possible that Gen Y's apparent inability to be patient is more a result of conditioning? I would suggest the latter.

Patience is not something we are born with, it is something that we learn. As children, we learn to wait for small things and realize that delaying gratification for these small things doesn't kill us. Gradually we learn to wait for bigger and bigger things until delaying gratification for months or even years is something we are willing and able to do as a result of the learned experiences of the past.

However, Generation Y has never really had to wait for anything. They have grown up with fast food, pre-prepared meals and lightning-fast internet. They tap their feet indignantly when a meal takes more than two minutes to cook in the microwave without realising that the same meal 20 years ago would have taken over an hour to cook using a conventional oven.

Just watch a Gen Y with a headache. Do they wait until it wears off, lie down for an hour or take an aspirin? No! They want fast-acting, super-strength Advil to deal with the headache NOW.

In the last 20 years, we have seen profound change in the underlying beliefs that shape society's collective approach to patience. We have shifted from the point where the default belief was that life was meant to be hard, to the other end of the spectrum where Gen Y have been raised to believe the very opposite – that life is meant to be *easy*. After all, such a belief is a mantra of the convenience-obsessed society which has shaped Gen Y.

The trouble with this underlying belief of course is that it is simply not accurate. Life is very often not easy, convenient or even fair. Loved ones pass away, exams are failed, relationships break up, global economic downturns occur.

In my work with Gen Y, it has become clear when life gets hard for this group who have been taught that it's meant to be easy, they tend to draw one of two conclusions;

1   There must be something wrong with my GOAL.

In other words, if life is meant to be easy and my life isn't, there must be something wrong with the path I have chosen.

Perhaps I am in the wrong job, the wrong relationship, or the wrong course. After all, if it was the right job, relationship or course, it would be easier than this.

From this perspective, setbacks, disappointments and frustrations are seen as reasons to change my goal in contrast to a traditional approach where hardships presented an opportunity for the goal to change me. In other words, if it's too difficult, Gen Y will often adjust their expectations, switch focus entirely or simply quit.

2   There must be something wrong with ME.

This second conclusion Gen Y tend to draw in the face of hardship is far more concerning than the first. I regularly urge parents, teachers and employers to keep an eye out for it in young people as it is often the breeding ground for mental health issues ranging from depression to suicidal tendencies.

To the same extent that Gen Y have been told that life is meant to be easy, this group have also been taught that life is meant to be exciting.

Older generations typically held the belief that 'normal' everyday life was largely mundane and that extreme emotions and experiences were the exception rather than the rule, In contrast, Gen Y have been raised on a steady diet of TV drama series and heavily edited 'reality' programs which capture only the ecstatic highs and devastating lows in people's lives. As a result, many young people have come to believe that normal everyday life for them ought to be much the same – dramatic.

I have witnessed first-hand the tendency for Gen Y to be most comfortable in the extreme highs and lows of life. For this group, it is when they are in between the extremes, when nothing is going on and when life gets boring that they become unsettled and may even start looking for ways to create drama.

With such an aversion to patience, delayed gratification and boredom, is it any wonder that Gen Y struggle to commit to college degrees and vo-tech courses? When faced with three to four years of investment without immediate return, a gap year or a job straight out of school can seem a far more palatable option.

The challenge for employers is to recognize that the pace and tempo of the workplace is often far too slow for this generation to get excited by or be engaged in. In the coming years, many organizations will need to consider redesigning the structures, processes and policies that slow progress and change if they are going to get the best out of this younger generation of workers.

That said, however, there is certainly a case for teaching Gen Y to adjust their expectations of the speed at which the real world works. As the old saying goes, we must prepare the child for the path, not simply the path for the child. Further still, it is critical that this young generation learn how to find meaning and contentment in the mundane seasons of life we all inevitably experience.

The good news is that it is possible to teach Gen Y to persist, endure and delay gratification even if these things may not come naturally to them. We'll talk more about how to go about this in section three.

4 COMMUNICATION

You can often tell a person's generation simply by the way in which they use just one piece of communication technology.

Can you guess what that might that be?

That's right… the cell phone!

Many Baby Boomers purchased their first cell phone out of a perceived fear: *Just in case my car breaks down one day, all alone on a long dark road, I'd better have one.* Of course, even if they did, one day, break down on that infamous secluded road, their cell phone would probably be of little use to them. Chances are they had forgotten to top up their prepaid credits, had no reception, or had left their cell at home!

It took two years for my brothers and I to convince my mom that it was okay to take her phone with her when she left the house. She thought it made more sense to leave the phone behind on the bench in the kitchen charging next to the home phone so she didn't waste the battery.

When we finally persuaded her that the cell phone would survive leaving the house, she insisted on keeping it in her handbag, *switched off* until she needed to make a call. When asked why she persisted in doing something so illogical, she would simply respond: *I don't want to be contactable all the time!*

I suspect that many Boomers share her sentiment! This is a generation who want their cell phones to act simply as phones. They don't want them to be video cameras, MP3 players and texting devices – they just want to use cells as phones when it suits them.

Then we have Generation X.

Xers embraced cell phones because they were a convenient tool. They love texting because it means they don't have to talk to anybody and can communicate with friends quickly and easily.

Finally, we come to Generation Y.

For them, a cell phone is not just a convenient tool – it is an extension of their identity. *How much bling has your phone got? What ring tone did you download last night?* For Generation Y a cell phone is a fashion accessory as much as it is a core necessity of daily living.

Recently, I was speaking at a youth leadership day for a group of seniors at a private high school. One of my sessions on the day was similar to the *Engaging Generation Y* presentation I deliver to business and parent audiences except that for this group I flipped it on its head and entitled the session *Why your parents are weird.*

As normal, I spent the first twenty minutes or so outlining each of the different generations and explaining their key differences. When I reached this point about attitudes to communication, however, I decided to ask the group a tongue-in-cheek rhetorical question. *'If you had to choose*

"TO GEN Y COMMUNICATION IS MORE ABOUT FUNCTION THAN IT IS ABOUT FORM."

between losing either your cell phone or your left leg, which would you go with?' They started to think. I could see students weighing up the two options in their minds. And then it happened – one of them shouted out: *'My leg!'*

I was speechless. He was serious!

That day gave me an even deeper insight into just how vital instantaneous communication is for Generation Y – it is core to their existence. If they haven't checked their messages for an hour, they are getting anxious – *'What if someone has broken up and I don't know?'*

Indicative of how widespread cell phone use is in this young group, by the middle of 2007 72% of 13 to 17 year olds owned a cell phone[66] and in one recent study over a third of those under 25 stated they couldn't live without their phone.[67]

Parents are often bemused and slightly concerned by the fact that their Gen Y son or daughter will rush home from school only to jump online and chat for hours to the same friends they have spent all day with. 'What could you possibly have to chat about?' parents will ask in frustration. If you have ever found yourself asking this very question, can I suggest that you've missed the point. It is not about *what* is being communicated, it is about the need for this generation to be *in communication* at all times. This need to be in communication is more than a strong desire or preference; it is almost a pathological addiction.

To see just how deeply ingrained the modern methods of communication are for this generation you need only look at the sub-dialect they have developed. Some call it *Gen-Y-nese* while to others it is known as *text-speak*. You have probably seen it featuring in everything from senior school essays to Mother's Day cards and even resumes!

Just for fun, try having a go at making sense of this message in Gen Y dialect: [68]

> *My smmr hols wr CWOT.*
> *B4, we usd 2 go 2 NY 2C*
> *my bro, his GF & thr 3 :-@ kds.*
> *FWIW, ILNY - its gr8. GTG, PAW*

How did you go? Did you figure out more than 60% of the words? If so, congratulations! You are well above average.

If you really struggled, however, let me translate it for you:

> *My summer holidays were a complete waste of time.*
> *Before, we used to go to New York to see my brother, his girlfriend and their three screaming kids.*
> *For what it's worth, I love New York – it's a great place.*
> *Got to go, parents are watching.*

Amazing, isn't it? The concept and methods of communication have changed so dramatically in just 15 years. Let's look at a comparison between our two generational paradigms to see the impact of such an evolution.

Established Generational Lens

For members of an established generation, communication is all about *form*. This group learned the rules of communicating by rote at school. They were marked based on how correctly they used grammar, punctuation and sentence construction. Correct communication, they were taught, was all about following the rules.

Our modern education systems tend to adopt a similar approach as evidenced by national literacy exams designed to evaluate, amongst other things, how 'correctly' our students are communicating.

Many Boomers and Builders often despair at the fact that the younger generation have taken less than ten years to destroy something that took centuries to build – the English language. They look at the way Generation Y uses text-speak, and wonder why they can't just write things the way they *should* – there's that word again!

This is seen especially in the business world where poor written communication skills can cost money and opportunities. One recent poll of business owners by *SmartCompany* revealed that almost 70% of employers are dissatisfied with their Gen Y employees' spelling and grammar.[69]

Many teachers are horrified when they learn that a number of government education departments around the world are beginning to adopt policies which specify they will now accept text language in their leaving certificate exams providing the examiner can understand the student was trying to say.

The battle lines in communication have certainly been drawn.

Generation Y Lens

In contrast with an established generational paradigm, to Generation Y communication is more about function than it is about form. It is about getting a message across in the cheapest, fastest and easiest way. They would argue that as long as you understand what they have said, why should it matter *how* they have said it?

Using the 'text-speak' example above, they would justify their use of abbreviations by asking why they would use 184 letters when they can use 72?

One Saturday afternoon my wife, Hailey, was marking some of her class's English essays when I noticed that she was being particularly harsh on one student's paper. There she was, armed with her

"EACH GENERATION TENDS TO DEFEND THE LANGUAGE OF THEIR PARENTS FROM THE LANGUAGE OF THEIR CHILDREN."

trusty red pen, crossing out words, circling sentences and furiously scribbling notes in the margins. As I watched her graffiti this student's work I innocently asked what the student had done so horrifically wrong.

She proceeded to show me numerous examples throughout the essay where the student had substituted full English words with text-style abbreviations. For example, instead of writing *'your'* this girl had simply written the abbreviation *'ur'*.

'We have been instructed not to accept any of these abbreviations from students,' Hailey said.

I thought about it for a minute and then asked, 'But did you get the message? Do you know what the student meant?'

'Yes, but that makes no difference as far as the school is concerned,' Hailey responded.

As I considered the implications of such an impasse, I wondered if Gen Y's way of communicating could actually be the next evolution in the English language. After all, we don't speak like Shakespeare did. Is it possible that each generation tends to defend the language of their parents from the language of their children?

While on the topic of Shakespeare, my colleague Mark McCrindle offers a humorous text-speak rendering of the famous balcony scene from Romeo and Juliet in his book *The ABC of XYZ*:

Romeo: R u awake? Want 2 chat?

Juliet: O Rom. Where4 art thou?

Romeo: Outside yr window.

Juliet: Stalker!

Romeo: Had to come. Feeling jiggy.

Juliet: B careful. My family h8 u.

Romeo: Tell me about it. What about u?

Juliet: 'm up for marriage f u are. Is tht a bit fwd?

Romeo: No. Yes. No. Oh, dsnt mat-r, 2moro @ 9?

Juliet: Luv U xxxx

Romeo: CU then xxxx[70]

Although there may be a compelling case for the argument that text message speak is simply part of the evolution of language, I do acknowledge that there are five significant implications of this streamlined and utilitarian approach to communication:

1. The Potential for Miscommunication

Despite the development of loosely defined text etiquette such as using capital letters for volume and face symbols for emotion, the potential for miscommunication in texting is enormous. One relationship counsellor reported to me recently that the first ground rule she sets in place when working with feuding couples is to forbid the use of text communication for a set time period due to the potential for conflict-causing misunderstandings.

2. The Erosion of Empathy

Researchers from the University of Michigan recently found that a reduction in face-to-face interactions is the primary reason today's students display 40% less empathy than students in the 1980s and 1990s.[71]

I would suggest this goes a long way to explaining why bullying (particularly online) has escalated in frequency and intensity over recent years even though today's postmodern students are more philosophically tolerant than their predecessors.

3. Changes in Physiology

This third very practical implication of Gen Y's methods of communication is seen in the fact that they are increasingly leaving essays unfinished in exams. Teachers report that this isn't because the students don't know the material but rather because their hands get so sore they can't physically write the quantities required.

I often joke that one solution could be to have students 'text' their essays in exams. Considering the average teenager sends 1,742 texts per month,[72] there ought to be no physiological deficiency in their thumbs!

4. Sleep Deprivation

Whether through texting, IM, Facebook or plain old phone calls, young people display an increasing unwillingness and aversion to switching off – especially at night when they need to be sleeping.

The lack of sleep in this generation has serious implications for behaviour, learning and mental health. One recent study of over 20,000 young people aged 17 to 24 found that those who slept less than five hours per night were three times more likely to develop mental health issues than those who had an adequate amount of sleep.[73]

Cell phone use aside, the issue of sleep patterns in teenagers is one that has attracted significant debate in education circles over recent years in relation to school start times. Even a young person who is not distracted from sleep by the technology designed to keep them in touch will find it difficult both to fall asleep and wake early – not because they are lazy but because they are not biologically wired to do so.

Citing research by renowned Stanford sleep expert William Dement, Prof. Jean Twenge suggests that young people generally find it difficult to fall asleep before 11.00pm or midnight and as such there may be very good reasons for schools to consider pushing back school-day start time.[74]

Obviously, technology distraction and addiction will exacerbate the issue of sleep loss but it is important to acknowledge that there are also biological factors to consider.

5. Shrinking Vocabulary

In 1950, the average 14 year old had a vocabulary of over 25,000 words in contrast to the average modern 14 year old whose vocabulary consists of just 10,000 words.[75] Even more startling is one recent study which found that the average young person uses only 800 different words each day.[76]

While many educators and parents worry that young people's limited vocabulary will significantly impair their employment prospects, I suspect the greatest impact of a shrinking vocabulary in Gen Y is in the way it affects their ability to communicate feelings and emotions both to themselves and others. In the absence of a vocabulary to adequately describe an emotion (i.e. I am feeling despondent, ecstatic, elated, overwhelmed, introspective), young people will tend to resort to more general and inadequate language for communicating emotions (i.e. life sucks, this is dumb, I'm over it etc).

The danger here is that being able to label and describe a complex emotion is the first step in processing it. Furthermore, if a young person lacks the ability to clearly communicate feelings, emotions and needs to others, they will resort to more base forms of communication such as verbal abuse or physical violence.

The differences between generational approaches to communication became acutely clear to me a few years ago when I was invited to form part of a televised debate on national TV lookingat the topic of modern-day manners and the evolution of what is socially acceptable and normal in communication.

In the course of our discussions, fellow panel members expressed their indignation that young people today seem to think it is appropriate to use very informal communication methods like text language in formal environments. Examples were given of young people cancelling or re-scheduling job interviews or calling in sick for work by sending a text message to their boss.

While older generations tend to perceive this as rude behavior, I suggested on air that this generation would be completely unaware that such a message could cause offense. To them, communicating in the easiest and fastest manner is just the way they have always done it.

Of course, writing for the audience and the occasion will always be necessary elements to consider for this younger generation moving forward. The ability to flex in and out of communication styles will be a vital lesson for Gen Y to learn in the coming years.

However, regardless of your personal opinion of Gen Y's language and methods of communicating, it is important not to underestimate the priority that this group place upon communication. They are communicating more and at a deeper level than any generation before them – especially the guys.

Sometimes when parents complain that they wish their children would communicate with them more, I jokingly suggest that they open a Facebook account or follow their kids on Twitter. That is where this generation does all its talking!

5 AFFIRMATION

Established Generational Lens

From the perspective of more traditional generations, the most important form of affirmation is an internal sense of personal pride and accomplishment from a job well done. From such a perspective, this intrinsic sense of affirmation is reason enough to apply oneself and to strive for excellence and achievement.

Naturally, whether someone else notices or gives me an award is secondary. It may be a nice bonus to receive acclaim and applause from others but such external affirmation is not a driving motivator.

Conversely, when criticism or constructive feedback is given by an external source, older generations have the ability to separate their performance from their personhood. They don't see constructive feedback as a personal attack but rather an opportunity to learn and grow no matter how uncomfortable, confronting or humiliating the process may be.

Generation Y Lens

By far the most common complaint I hear from employers and managers of Gen Y is that this young group seem to need to be affirmed for everything they do. 'Why do we have to congratulate Gen Y for simply turning up to work?' I am often asked by frustrated bosses.

In contrast with older generations, Gen Y crave *external* affirmation for their performance, development and effort. In one recent study, 60% of Gen Y employees reported wanting to receive feedback from their managers on a daily basis and 35% wanted feedback multiple times a day.[77]

Such a heavy reliance on external praise and feedback in Gen Y seems to be a key factor in the development of the 'if no-one is going to notice, why bother trying at all' attitude so prevalent in this group.

I suspect that this need for external feedback in Gen Y is actually what drives their use of social media too. For this group, social media is not simply about sharing and building community online. Rather, it is about gaining feedback, affirmation and validation. If the purpose of social media were simply to share, young people wouldn't update their status on Facebook and then check back 20 seconds later to see what the response had been (i.e. did people click 'like' or make a comment).

Gen Y seem to have a pathological compulsion to get feedback on every thought, opinion, feeling or experience. It is not simply enough to enjoy a beautiful sunset, realize something profound for the first time or discover a new favorite pizza topping – everything has to be shared with the world in order to gain validation.

Naturally, this has earned Gen Y the reputation of being the most narcissistic and self absorbed generation of teenagers in history. Some would suggest that such a reputation is well founded. According to one study, the number of university or college students who rate 'high' on the Narcissistic Personality Inventory (NPI) has increased by almost 70% between 1987 and 2006.[78]

What is interesting to watch is how Gen Y respond when the opposite of external praise and affirmation are given. Stories abound of young people simply folding at the knees, dissolving into tears or violently lashing out when criticism or constructive feedback is given. One teacher reported a student's devastation when she was asked to review her work and do a second draft – 'why do you hate me so much' the student asked.

Compared to older generations, it appears that Gen Y are less able to separate their performance from their personhood. As a result, any negative feedback is seen as a personal attack.

This certainly begs a question: if Gen Y have been raised in the era of self esteem, why does everything seem to come crashing down like a house of cards at the first hint of criticism and negative feedback? I believe it is because one of the greatest myths of the last three decades is that self esteem can be given or bestowed when it simply cannot.

Picking up on this theme, Prof. Jean Twenge suggests that true self esteem is an outcome, not a cause. Eminent psychologist Martin Seligman agrees having widely criticized self-esteem programs and arguing that a sense of self esteem that is not based on a tangible accomplishment or the development of a new skill does not serve children well in the longer term.

While parents, teachers and employers can and must give encouragement, affirm progress and build confidence in young people, true self esteem is always an internally driven thing. If we are to set Gen Y up for long term success, it is critical we foster a healthy sense of self pride in them that is linked to overcoming challenges, pushing the limits of personal achievement and persisting through setbacks.

Again, we will discuss this further in section three.

6 THE FUTURE

Established Generational Lens

The career mission and view of the future for a traditional generation was linear and clear – get a good education, a safe, secure job and specialize in that one job, or at least that one industry, till retirement at age 65. If at retirement you have proven yourself to be a loyal company man or company woman, you may be lucky enough to receive a gold watch on your final day of work.

Ironically, although many Boomers haven't themselves had careers that follow this paradigm, it is still the expectation they can unconsciously have for their children as it was the expectation their parents had for them.

Parents who have this traditional mind-set will often worry that their son or daughter hasn't yet figured out what career path they would like to pursue by age 16. They fear that their child will be left behind if they don't work towards getting a head-start straight out of high school. *'Why won't my son or daughter get serious and start thinking about their future?'* I am often asked.

Older generations point with bewilderment to young people who have trained for years in a certain field then suddenly decide to take an entirely new direction five years into their working life. They will ask why someone would throw away a good career to go in search of a new horizon.

The answer to this question lies in the fact that Generation Y has a very different view of the future.

Generation Y Lens

For Gen Ys, the future is an exciting and uncertain maze of opportunities, contingencies and pathways. 'Career' is one long resume-building process.

In my early days of working with students, one of the most popular topics requested by guidance counselors and principals was goal setting. Being largely of the Boomer generation, these teachers felt it was necessary and important that their students develop clear plans for the future.

In putting together my initial session on goal setting, I did what every inexperienced communicator does – I copied what I had seen work for others in the past. In every goal-setting workshop I had attended, the presenter invariably asked audience members to set out a five-year plan and work backwards. The only trouble was when I started to ask students where they wanted to be in five years time all I got were blank stares.

It didn't take me long to figure out what wasn't working. This generation had absolutely no idea where they wanted to be in five years time. More to the point, they were in no hurry to figure it out.

The reality is most Gen Ys don't know what they are going to do next weekend. They will wait till all the text messages or Facebook invites come in on a Friday night and then choose the best option on offer. The aim is to keep one's options open until all the contingencies are laid out.

This is precisely the way Gen Y approach their future as well.

I was speaking to a girl after a recent goal-setting session and asked her what she intended to do when she finished school. Her response was one I have heard many times since from Gen Ys. It started with the words: *Well, my ambition for this week is…*

To an older generation this sort of comment may well be viewed as flippant, unfocused and inappropriate for a young woman making serious career decisions. It's important to note, however, that our schools and education system have told Gen Y for the last 15 years that they will have multiple majors at college and numerous careers in

"FOR GEN Y, THE FUTURE IS AN EXCITING AND UNCERTAIN MAZE OF OPPORTUNITIES, CONTINGENCIES AND PATHWAYS."

their lives. Why are we now surprised that they believe this to be true? Young people today are in no hurry to decide what they are going to spend the rest of their lives doing because they figure that they have the rest of their lives to do just that.Their focus is on developing interchangeable skills rather than narrowing down their options and choosing one specific career.

Such an aversion to planning for the future extends to education as well. In America, the average college student takes 6 years to graduate either because they are widening their options by choosing double and triple majors or simply changing their major multiple times mid course.[79]

Having grown up in a time of rapid technological change, Gen Y are fully aware that the future is uncertain and constantly evolving. As American educator Karl Fisch suggests;

We are currently preparing students for jobs that don't yet exist, using technologies that haven't been invented yet, in order to solve problems we don't even know are problems yet.[80]

Bearing this prediction in mind, perhaps Gen Y's approach to the future is both appropriate and realistic.

I find it humorous that career and guidance counselors will boldly inform students that the jobs they will have in the future are yet to exist but then in the next breath tell students that it is important to sit down and work out a detailed career plan.

For Gen Y, the word 'plan' has little relevance whereas the word 'prepare' makes much more sense. Young people's mentality is that locking in medium-to-long-term plans is both futile and potentially limiting. As such, this group's focus is on being prepared for the future by developing interchangeable skills rather than narrowing down their options and planning one specific career path. If you are a teacher or parent, it is vital to adopt the mind-set of 'preparing' rather than 'planning' if you are going to engage young people in thinking about the future.

In addition to the changes Gen Y has seen and will continue to see in the technology that drives our world, this group is also entering a career climate where the concept of work has changed. The emergence of 'portfolio careers' has resulted directly in the shift we have seen towards a casualization of the workforce. Long gone are the days where it was normal to have one full-time job. According to a Newsweek article published in January 2009, the number of people working part-time in the USA almost doubled from 4.5 million to nearly 8 million in just 12 months.[81]

Generation Y's expectation of a career future that is varied, unpredictable and flexible has profound implications on the way this group approaches our next area of paradigm rift. Of the nine areas of rift that we cover in this section, the next area is the one causing most friction and frustration in businesses right across the Western world when it comes to Gen Y.

That area? Loyalty, of course.

7 LOYALTY

Established Generational Lens

In a bygone era, loyalty was an inherent part of the job contract. The very fact that an employer had given you a job required that you give loyalty in return. Loyalty was almost seen as a moral obligation to one's boss.

This attitude often extended into an employee's life outside of work too. For example, if the company you worked for was criticized in conversation at a weekend BBQ, older generations felt an obligation to defend the company they worked for.

When members of the established generations got a job they would describe it as *joining a new company*. The inference was that you were, in a sense, joining a family that would look after you and provide financial security and you, in return, would show them loyalty and a strong work ethic.

For traditional generations, loyalty to and longevity with an employer were seen as directly related. One was evidence of the other. It was not unusual to stay working for an employer for ten or more years and to wear this long service as a badge of pride.

Generation Y Lens

It may come as no great surprise to you and may well be the understatement of the decade, but Gen Y tend not to approach loyalty in the same way their parents and employers do. When this generation get a job, they don't 'join' a company, they simply work for them. Work is just something they do. It is not a 'family' they become part of, and they will never go as far as entrusting their future security to a boss.

Gen Y start a new job with the clear (but often unexpressed) goal of staying around just long enough to learn, gain skills, and develop contacts before moving on to the next opportunity that offers them more. Loyalty and longevity are simply no longer part of the equation.

As a dramatic illustration of this point, one corporate client I worked with showed me their internal HR statistics in relation to loyalty and longevity across generations. Baby Boomers, they told me, had an average length of tenure of just over ten years. Gen X stayed around for 4.2 years on average before moving on. Their Gen Y employees, however, had an average length of tenure of just 17 months!

It would appear that this company is by no means a unique case. Researcher Mark McCrindle cites data showing that Gen Y are three times more likely to change jobs in any given year than their Baby Boomer counterparts[82] and similar statistics from the US show that the average length of tenure amongst Gen Ys is just 2.6 years.[83]

As I work with corporate clients helping them shape their culture and processes to be more engaging to Gen Y, I hear story after story of the same experience. Younger generations are not necessarily loyal to their employers and many companies can't seem to understand why. I suspect there are three reasons:

A) Generation Y have grown up in an era of unparalleled economic prosperity

As described in the previous section, Gen Y have grown up in an era of great prosperity where jobs were plentiful and employees were in a more powerful bargaining position than they had been for decades.

Prior to the advent of the Global Financial Crisis (GFC), all Gen Y ever heard the media talk about were the skills shortage, the aging workforce, and record-breaking low unemployment figures. As a result, this group developed a perception that jobs were plentiful and easy to come by. If they didn't get what they wanted in their current position, they would simply leave because they figured that they could walk down the street and find another job that would probably have given them what they wanted and they may have even secured higher pay or a promotion in the process.

This attitude stood in stark contrast to that of their parents who were often loyal not out of virtue but through fear. Many older generation workers stayed, and continue to stay, working in positions that they don't like simply because they fear that if they leave they may not find another job as good. For this group, the 'devil you know is better than the one you don't' and staying put often seems the wisest and safest option.

Of course, the advent of the Global Financial Crisis (GFC) has dramatically altered the labor market and somewhat knocked the wind out of Gen Y's bold, confident sails. Accordingly, Gen Ys have started to curb their flippant job-hopping ways – for now. I suspect that the recent displays of 'loyalty' and longevity that employers are seeing in their Gen Y staff are little more than this group playing the game. They may stay put in the short to medium term while times are tough, but as soon as the economy picks up and unemployment levels begin to fall, watch the carousel of Gen Y job rotations again start to spin.

While many employers secretly hope that the current downturn will go a long way to putting Gen Y firmly 'in their place' I suspect that while it may knock some of the hard edges off this group, their fundamental paradigm around their rights and responsibilities in relation to employment will remain much the same as it was in the pre-GFC era.

B) They have not had loyalty modeled to them

Although Gen Y has only recently discovered what society-wide economic adversity feels like, they did witness how the last downturn affected their parents. As young children, many of them saw their parents get outsourced, right-sized, downsized and justified out of positions by those same employers their parents had been loyal to for years.

Seeing how companies treated their parents, Gen Ys have a rather cynical view of loyalty towards employers. Amazingly, it is often the same companies that laid off their parents 20 years ago that are now complaining that Gen Y won't show loyalty.

C) Loyalty is no longer seen as necessary for career advancement and may well even be unhelpful

A far cry from the days when 25 years with the same employer indicated commitment, persistence and character, recruiters are now telling me about the curse of experience when it comes to young people applying for positions. If, for example, a young person's resume shows that they worked in their last position for more than four years, they are now being asked what is wrong with them – *why did you stay there so long*?

It is no wonder then that Gen Y have adopted the belief that loyalty is not only unwarranted but also potentially *unhelpful* for career advancement. Loyalty and longevity are now seen as negatives and taken as an indication that you may lack creativity, drive and flexibility!

It seems that many employers want to have their cake and eat it too. They want their current employees, in whom they have invested training, money and time, to make a commitment to staying for the long term. At the same time though, they look for young staff who can demonstrate flexibility in the variety of positions they have held and

"SEEING HOW COMPANIES TREATED THEIR PARENTS, GEN Y HAVE A RATHER CYNICAL VIEW OF LOYALTY TOWARDS EMPLOYERS."

rotated through in their relatively short careers. Then, on top of all this, they expect employees to be loyal even though job security is not assured and full-time positions may not even be on offer.

All too often, today's employers want all the benefits of a part-time, flexible workforce without any of the associated costs. Furthermore, they bemoan the fact that Gen Ys don't show loyalty and yet they offer no other reason for doing so than that they *should*.

Indeed, the whole concept of loyalty to employers has changed dramatically in the last three decades. It is not enough to simply wish that we could return to the good old days when employees stayed with you for life. The modern-day mobile and transient workforce of young people creates a number of exciting opportunities for businesses and employers if they can recognize the shift and respond to it. The challenge for organizations is to create cultures, structures and processes that attract this group. I will talk more about this in section three.

8 WORK ETHIC

Established Generational Lens

Through an established generational lens, work ethic is often intrinsically linked to identity. Work is integral to gaining a sense of fulfillment, purpose and status. Older generations often tend to live to work. Not only is work expected to be hard, but getting ahead requires commitment, sacrifice and imbalance. Many older workers believe that life should fit in around work and any notion of balance is reserved for retirement – the 20 years of no work that comes after 40 years of hard work.

Established generations have such a strong sense of work ethic because they see having a good job as a privilege. If an employee is lucky enough to have a good job (one characterized by high pay, benefits, predictability and security) they will tend to work as hard as necessary to ensure they keep that job.

Often workplace cultures have developed around an established generational approach to work ethic. An employee's contribution and worth is often gauged by the *quantity* of hours they work and the sacrifice they have made. As a result, however, this group's commitment to the job has often come at a great cost. Family life, leisure time and health have almost always been given a lower priority than being a committed 'company man' (or woman).

Generation Y Lens

Older generations often criticise Gen Ys for being lazy and uncommitted when it comes to their work ethic. What they fail to realize is that younger generations are not necessarily lazy but simply approach work with a different mind-set.

I was recently speaking with an apprenticeships coordinator responsible for placing trainees and apprentices with businesses in her local area. She is responsible for placing trainees and apprentices with businesses in the region. She described to me how her greatest challenge is mediating between bosses and trainees who often have very different expectations of work.

One employer had taken on three apprentices in the last year and fired all of them. When she arranged to meet with this employer and discuss what wasn't working, he described the problem as being 'these lazy young people' who turn up on the stroke of nine and down tools at 5 o'clock, regardless of whether they have finished a job or not.

Clearly exasperated, he asked 'What is wrong with today's youth? How dare they walk out without finishing what they are doing? It means that someone else, probably me, will have to stay back late to get things finished.'

To understand why Generation Y's approach to work ethic is different to that of previous generations, you only have to look at their parents. Young people have seen the heart attacks, strokes, broken marriages and stress caused by a lack of work-life balance in their parents' lives. As a result, they are resolved not to do the same. For them, work-life balance is not simply a nice idea – it is a top priority.

This generation places such a high value on relationships that they will not easily forego events and occasions with relational significance just because their bosses need them to stay back at work. Many would rather lose a job than stay and lose the flexibility of their life outside work. Somewhat surprisingly, this attitude seems to have prevailed even in the face of economic downturn and adversity. A recent US study showed that even at the height of the GFC, young people were turning down 'unsuitable' job offers at the same rate they were in the pre-GFC boom times.[84]

It is not that Gen Ys are as lazy as their reputation would suggest. Work for them just has a very different priority as part of their life than it does for their bosses. Gen Ys work to live. For them, work fits in around their lives, not

> "GEN Y WORKS TO LIVE. FOR THEM, WORK FITS IN AROUND THEIR LIVES, NOT VICE VERSA."

vice versa. They work to fund their lifestyle and find less of their identity and status in their work output than their parents.

For Gen Y, a good job is not seen as a privilege but as a right. Furthermore, what constitutes a *good job* for this group is different from previous generations. Bestselling American authors Bruce Tuglan and Dr. Carolyn Martin suggest that the compensation drivers for Gen Y tend to be flexibility, respect, variety and the opportunity for further training as opposed to high pay and job security.[85]

The key challenge in motivating Gen Y to give their best at work is to recognize what drives them and create flexible work cultures that value collaboration, creative input and empowerment. Gen Y will work hard for organizations that provide such environments.

9 LEARNING

Established Generational Lens

When older generations were at school, 'chalk and talk' was the teaching method of the day. The ability to memorize and regurgitate information was a vital skill for academic success.

Children sat in rigid rows of wooden desks inside schools that looked vastly different to the modern learning environments being built today.

Teachers were feared and revered. The teacher was the final and highest authority. Questioning this authority meant detention, lines, or even worse, the cane!

In this era, learning for learning's sake was a valuable endeavor. Universities and colleges were filled with students who simply had a thirst for knowledge.

When older generations studied at home, they would sit at desks in silence and solitude memorising the information they would need to regurgitate to their teachers.

Generation Y Lens

Gen Y's mind-set in relation to school, education and learning is vastly different to that of older generations. For them, education is all about tangible outcomes. If what they are learning is not in some clear way connected with a skill that will help them move ahead in their careers or lives, they are simply not interested.

I would suggest that very few Gen Ys are studying at a university level out of a thirst for knowledge. Rather, today's colleges are filled with students who are focused on discovering a vocational direction, getting a degree and then getting out into the 'real world' as quickly as possible to get on with their careers.

Added to this, the *methods* and *style* of learning for Generation Y have also changed. When this group study they tend not to sit in silence at desks in their room as their parents did. More likely you will find them lying on the floor typing on the laptop, iPod in their ears, watching TV in the background, and all the while writing an English essay!

In case you thought young people like the above were an exception rather than the rule, one recent large-scale study found that three quarters of Gen Y students reported using instant messaging while doing their homework.[86]

Older generations look at this and are bewildered. 'How can children these days learn anything with all that noise, clutter and distraction?' they will ask. It is a good question and one that need not and ought not be rhetorical. American educational researcher Alan Simon has coined a term for the ability of Generation Y to use multiple media simultaneously with ease. He calls it *techno-tasking*. In a 2005 article for *The School Administrator*, Simon warns that the ability of students to multi-task with technology carries major ramifications for classroom instruction and decision making.[87]

While younger learners have short attention spans and low concentration, they can take in information at incredibly fast speeds, and are well adapted to a world overloaded with information and 'noise'. By the time an average Gen Y has reached their twenties, they will have spent over 20,000 hours on the internet and over 10,000 hours playing video games of

"THREE QUARTERS OF GEN Y STUDENTS REPORT USING INSTANT MESSAGING WHILE DOING THEIR HOMEWORK."

some kind.[88] This is on top of the countless hours they have spent watching television programs where images, themes and sounds change every few seconds in case it becomes too boring for the viewer. Harvard Medical School Associate Professor Michael Rich suggests that all this conditioning has created a generation of young people whose brains are simply "wired differently."[89]

As a compelling example of this change, Mark McCrindle points to the fact that when the Dunn, Dunn & Price Learning Style Inventory was first developed in 1978, 70% of high school students were shown to be auditory learners. Although this learning style may not have been their natural one, McCrindle suggests that learners had conformed to the 'chalk and talk' teaching approach of the day. He goes on to point out that only 30% of students today are auditory learners and that this change has been heavily influenced the world young people have grown up in.[90]

Following a recognition of this shift in learning styles and needs, a number of schools I have worked with in recent years have developed classroom policies which now allow the use of iPods during lessons. During follow-up workshops with these groups, teachers report that students are far more settled and focused when they are allowed to listen to music during personal work time than if there were silence.

Despite this growing acceptance of iPods in the classroom, debate rages as to whether students really can technotask as well as they believe they can. Prof. Sherry Turkle who has been teaching at MIT in Cambridge for over 30 years has watched students change and evolve over that time with a degree of concern. She believes that young people have done themselves a disservice by believing that a multitasking learning environment will serve their best purposes.[91]

Prof. Turkle is not alone in her fears. In his book *CrazyBusy*, psychiatrist Edward Hallowell worries that many young people today are exhibiting symptoms similar to attention deficit disorder due to the technology they are exposed to. He points to a generation of shallow and distracted learners who lack the ability to focus.[92]

Weighing into the debate, the head of cognitive neuroscience at the American Institute of Neurological Disorders and Strokes concedes that while Gen Y may be able to adapt to multitasking behaviours due to long term conditioning, this may well come at the cost of creativity, inventiveness and productivity.[93]

However, there are others who point to the tangible and positive impacts of Gen Y's digital immersion. Don Tapscott points to the fact that young video game players have highly developed spatial skills, improved hand-eye co-ordination, faster response times and enhanced abilities for divided attention. Furthermore, he points to the benefits of younger people being able to quickly switch tasks and find information on the internet because of the experience they have had doing so throughout their lives. In short, he points to a generation who are 'incredibly flexible, adaptable and multimedia savvy.' [94]

While this debate over the impact of multimedia on learning will likely continue for years to come, the anecdotal evidence I am hearing from thousands of teachers and parents is clear: Gen Y can and do learn perfectly well with much of the noise that previous generations may have found distracting.

My advice is to only enforce the silent learning environment approach if the young person is an extreme auditory learner or when they are studying in a way that is designed to simulate exam conditions (i.e. writing practice essays or doing past papers). In these instances, it would probably be a good idea for them to practice working in silence as it is the environment they will need to perform well in on the day.

In saying this, however, I do feel that some of the concerns held by experts over multimedia use are very valid. It is important to recognize the difference between noise and interruptions. Being able to work and learn effectively with an iPod in your ears is very different to being able to concentrate and think critically or creatively while being interrupted every three seconds by Instant Messenger.

Despite the protests and assertions from young people that they can still work perfectly well despite interruption, research does indicate that today's students have a higher personal estimation of their ability to cope with interruptions than is actually the case.[95]

As you are hopefully beginning to see, generational paradigms have an enormous effect on the way we behave and the mind-set with which we approach the world.

The challenge now is to work towards closing the rifts that separate us. Naturally this effort must be made by both sides if it is going to be sustainable and effective. However, for the purposes of our discussions I want to spend the final section focussing on some strategies that you as a parent, teacher or employer can use to better engage Generation Y.

THE 'NEW' RULES OF ENGAGEMENT

3

These symbols indicate that the chapter
will be of most relevance to:

E EMPLOYERS

T TEACHERS

P PARENTS

In military terms, rules of engagement are directives that determine the limitations and circumstances under which forces partake in combat. Or, to put it more simply, rules of engagement set out what to do when you come into contact with 'the other side'.

While I am not promoting the attitude that generations are at war with each other or that we should see each other as the enemy, I do think we can borrow some ideas from this military concept.

What I mean is that when you encounter or have to work with the younger generation in your daily life, it is important to have a blueprint for understanding, relating, and engaging across the gap.

This is the focus of section three. Building on a solid understanding of the cross-generational issues at play, I now want to help you develop an effective response to Generation Y.

You may remember some of the words I listed in the introduction that are related to the definition of 'engagement' – words like *attraction*, *connection* and *commitment*. Let's look at how these three things can be achieved with Gen Y. Whether you are an employer trying to recruit, manage and retain staff, or a teacher or parent trying to get a message through and build rapport with this group, my goal is that by the end of this section, you will be armed with some practical tools, strategies and ideas that will help you move from 'estranging' to 'engaging' Gen Y.

What is the secret to engaging Generation Y?

Many experts would suggest that as far as teaching is concerned, the answer to this question lies in an effective use of technology. They would suggest that high-tech classrooms and teaching programs stand the best chance of attracting and connecting with Generation Y. The problem with this approach is that it leaves most, apart from a few tech-savvy teachers and parents, with a profound and unwarranted sense of inadequacy.

> "WHILE TECHNOLOGY HAS A DEFINITE ROLE TO PLAY, IT IS ONLY A TOOL – AND NOT EVEN THE MOST IMPORTANT TOOL – FOR ENGAGING GENERATION Y."

I would argue that while technology has a definite role to play, it is only a tool – and not even the most important tool – for engaging Generation Y. Rather than simply relying on 'high-tech' approaches to attracting, teaching and raising this group, I have found that it is the 'high touch' strategies that work best.

Over the course of this section I will outline eight different rules or strategies that will help you engage Generation Y. I have used them in my own work with young people and have seen them implemented by thousands of parents, teachers and employers with great success.

Before we launch headlong into these, however, I want to acknowledge two deliberate ironies in entitling these strategies and this book *The 'New' Rules of Engagement*.

The first irony is that, while I have called these ideas 'rules', the strategies I will outline here are not in fact rules at all – they are principles. The difference between rules and principles is that while rules compel people externally through force, threat or punishment to do what is deemed right, principles describe patterns and natural laws in order to internally motivate behavior.

Secondly, these ideas are by no means 'new'. In fact, the keys for engaging Generation Y are so timeless that you could almost dismiss them as common sense. However, as the 18th century author Samuel Johnson said: *People need to be reminded more often than they need to be instructed.*

I firmly believe this to be true. With that in mind, let's be reminded together.

CHAPTER NINE
PUT RELATIONSHIP BEFORE ROLE

A few years ago I was invited to speak at an education conference that had been given the theme of *Improving Student Engagement* When I received the conference agenda a couple of days before the event, I was excited to learn that the speaker who would be presenting before me was actually going to be a student. I remember thinking: 'What a novel concept, having a student speak at a conference designed to help teachers better understand today's students!'

This young girl, Melissa, spoke for just over 30 minutes about the things that she and her friends found engaging in a teacher. While she offered a number of valuable insights, I was particularly struck by one thing she said: 'The teachers that my friends and I connect with are the ones who treat us like *people*, not just students.'

The room was silent. For some teachers there that day, this seemed like common sense. And yet it was a timely reminder considering common sense is not necessarily common practice. For many of the audience, however, it became clear that this notion was an uncomfortable one. This is not surprising when you realize that many of today's educators were taught in teachers college that if they had any hope of gaining the respect of their students they must not laugh, smile or show any hint of their 'humanness' for at least their first three months at a new school! Still today, many teachers believe that their role in the classroom is defined by the professional distance they maintain between themselves and their students. Furthermore, many employers and parents subscribe to a similar belief.

Historically, authority in its various forms was seen as *separation*. Under such a mind-set, those in authority established and maintained their power by separating themselves from those they were responsible for. In the void created by this separation, the goal was to develop a level of fear and intimidation to ensure compliance and maintain discipline.

This approach to leadership and management is commonly known as 'Power and Control'. It comes straight out of the industrial revolution and although much of the corporate world officially threw it out the window in the early 1990s, many organizations, most schools and countless homes still operate under a Power and Control mind-set.

I realized the extent to which Power and Control is still alive and well in sections of the business community on my first day working for a large IT firm after graduating from college.

I arrived on Monday morning to discover that the only parking available for my fellow workmates and me was in a back alleyway where cars were frequently broken into and vandalized. The directors, however, each had a labeled car space near the front door where they parked their luxury vehicles. As I walked in the front doors, it became even more obvious where I fitted in. To my left were the sparkling glass-encased offices of the management team, complete with gold-framed name plates on the closed doors. I was shown my desk at the centre of a maze of beige cubicles otherwise known as the 'chicken pen'. Going to the kitchen to make myself a coffee, it was reinforced once again where I fitted into the scheme of things. Placed neatly above the basin in the lunchroom was a printed sign reminding users to clean up after

"GENERATION Y HAVE INDEED TYPIFIED THE OLD SAYING: I DON'T CARE HOW MUCH YOU KNOW UNTIL I KNOW HOW MUCH YOU CARE."

themselves. It started with the words, 'Attention Management and Staff'. It was clear; there was a separation between management and the rest of us.

Such a separation of role and relationship in the workplace has often been codified in corporate culture. In his book *The ABC of XYZ*, Mark McCrindle quotes a passage from an etiquette guide written in 1959 as an example of how this was done:

If an employee is summoned to the employer's room, he must remain standing until his chief indicates a seat. At the conclusion of the interview he must leave as quietly as possible, closing the door gently after him. If an employee has a need to send a letter to his chief he should commence it with the words 'Dear sir' and conclude it with the words 'Yours Obediently'.[96]

Power and Control however is not just limited to workplaces and schools. On the home front, many parents make futile efforts to continue to hide behind familiar roles and labels. The 'do as I say, not as I do' approach to dictating behavior was once a parent's get-out-of-jail-free card – it covered a multitude of sins and seemed ample justification for inconsistency and double standards. The answer to the 'Why?' question was simply 'because I said so.' With today's generation of young people, however, a separation between the role of employer, parent or teacher, and the identity of the individual in that role, simply doesn't work.

Of course, none of this is to suggest that roles are redundant. The role of teachers, parents and employers in discipline and accountability is vital. Relationships, however, must come before this and any other role. As boys education expert, Ian Lillico, attests: *Today's students learn teachers, not subjects*. Whether you are teaching and leading this group in the classroom, the home or the workplace, I can assure you that your students, children and employees are learning *you* and not what you are trying to teach them. The relationship you build with this group is the most important ingredient to engagement. It is, in fact, the foundation. To this end, I often encourage teachers with the advice of a wise colleague: students won't necessarily remember what you teach them, but they'll always remember how you treat them.

Generation Ys have indeed typified the old saying: *I don't care how much you know until I know how much you care.*

This begs the question – what *type* of relationship is Generation Y looking for? Do they want you to get down to their level? Do they want you to be like *them*? The short answer is, no.

Every now and again you will see it – a teacher, parent or manager who decides that in an effort to connect with young people they will start dressing like them and using their slang. Unfortunately, these efforts are tragic for two reasons – they look ridiculous and they don't work.

This generation don't want you to be like them. As Tim Elmore suggests, kids are looking for parents to be leaders rather than servants, groupies or cheerleaders.[97] They don't want you to be their best friend or their peer. Rather, they respond to and connect with employers, teachers and parents who build rapport with them by being two things – authentic and interested.

A **AUTHENTIC**

Gen Ys want you to be you. When I ask this group who the adults are that they feel a connection with, the pattern of their responses is clear. They love the teacher who is a dag but can be honest about it. They love the manager who is upfront about making mistakes and humble enough to admit when they are wrong. They love the parent who doesn't pretend to have the answer to every single question.

This generation has a finely tuned 'BS meter'. (If you are not sure what BS means, ask a Gen Y!) Masks, insincerity and 'fake-ness' will never cut it. When young people detect even the slightest hint of inauthenticity, hypocrisy or double standards, the shutters come straight down on trust, respect and rapport.

Interestingly, this group don't relate to the slick, polished and professional performances that their Boomer parents do. As evidenced by Gen Y's addiction to reality TV, they love people and things that are raw, random and real.

A few years ago I watched a fascinating televised debate looking at leadership and gender equity in politics and business. The panel consisted of a number of notable older women in high-powered roles but had the curious inclusion of a 24-year old Gen Y who was a political science major.

The debate started by looking at issues such as the impact of the glass ceiling for women and paid maternity leave but quickly moved on to the more philosophical topic of what leadership actually meant. It was fascinating to hear each of the panel members offering different definitions of the traits and abilities required in a good leader.

When it finally came time for the Gen Y panel member to speak you could have heard a pin drop. What would she say? What exactly is it that the younger generation is looking for in their leaders? She began by describing how disconnected young people feel from many of today's politicians. Asked why this was the case and what would help leaders reconnect with a younger generation, there were four characteristics that came up repeatedly in her answer: *authentic*, *honest*, *vulnerable* and *real*. Her response was met with nods and sporadic applause by younger audience members. I suspect that this panel member spoke the mind of an entire generation that evening.

Older generations have become highly skilled in the art of ensuring that one's outward appearance is composed and in control at all times, regardless of what is going on behind the scenes.

From this perspective, the idea of being honest and authentic, especially with the young people in your charge, is unthinkable.

If you are part of this group the liberating truth is that young people don't want to see that you live a perfect and faultless life; they want to know that you live a real life. They love to see you go through a challenge and struggle with an issue. This is not out of some sadistic desire but is motivated by the connection brought about through shared experience. They want

"IF YOU ARE AIMING TO CONNECT WITH YOUNG PEOPLE, VULNERABILITY AND HONESTY WILL ALWAYS GO A LONG WAY."

to see how you deal with a Monday, a setback, a success, a personal crisis and most of all, the mundane-ness of normal everyday life. If you are aiming to connect with young people, vulnerability and honesty will always go a long way.

When attending a graduation ceremony at my old high school recently I noticed a considerable difference in the atmosphere of the school I had attended just eight years earlier. Looking around, it seemed that the students weren't just politely tolerant of their teachers; they actually appeared to like them. There was a sense of rapport and community that I never felt as a student.

When I asked some of the teachers what had changed, it became clear that a concerted effort had been made to build this culture. While there were a number of initiatives that had been effective in achieving this goal there was one event that came up in almost every conversation. Earlier that year the Year 12 students had taken the initiative of organizing a fundraising event called *Dancing with the Staff*. Modeled on the popular television show of a similar name, this event saw students pair up with a teacher, choose a song, choreograph a routine, spend months rehearsing and finally perform in front of the whole school. The stories that came out of this day were hilarious, to say the least. From the costumes and the moves to the trips and falls, *Dancing with the Staff* was an event that students and teachers alike described as 'one of the best days this school has ever had'.

> "TO BUILD RAPPORT WITH GEN Y, THE KEY IS TO BE INTERESTED AND IMPRESSED... BY THEM."

It was clear, however, that this day was more than just fun and frivolity. *Dancing with the Staff* seemed to have been a significant step forward in breaking down the barrier between teachers and students. Suddenly, students saw teachers as real people who would have a go, even if it made them look silly. Likewise, teachers had the opportunity to work with students on a project that took them out of their classroom roles and built rapport and connections that carried over into the classroom. The result was a wonderfully positive change in the culture of the school.

In saying all this, though, vulnerability and honesty should always be approached with good judgment, common sense and an awareness of appropriate boundaries. You must be vulnerable from a position of strength and not neediness or weakness. The classroom or the workplace should never become a confessional or a forum for group therapy. That said, the basic message is: *don't be afraid to let down your guard (and your hair) with Generation Y. If you do, they'll love you for it*.

B INTERESTED

There is a sense among many adults I speak with that to connect with this younger generation you need to be *interesting* and *impressive*. In other words, if you are not cool, fascinating and 'hip' then they won't want to connect with you.

In actual fact the very opposite is true – to build rapport with Gen Y, the key is to be *interested* and *impressed...* by them.

While this generation doesn't necessarily want you to be interested in the same things they are, *showing* an interest in them and their lives is a powerful relationship-building tool.

Following a recent *Engaging Generation Y* session I ran for a government education group, one older teacher was excited to tell me that my presentation had just put language around a strategy she had stumbled across a number of years before. Having worked in schools for more than 30 years, this teacher had noticed a change in the 'clientele' about ten years ago. Experimenting with a number of strategies to build connections with the new breed of students, she found the one that worked best was to develop the habit of being actively and deliberately interested. Having been asked repeatedly by colleagues for years what her secret was when it came to building rapport with students, she now realized that it was simply the level of interest she showed.

The teacher described to me how she regularly tries to discover something of interest or concern for each of her students and then makes a personal commitment to ask them about it. Sometimes it is about a movie they have seen or a sporting event they competed in on the weekend. Perhaps it is discussing the latest gossip from Hollywood or even asking after a sick parent.

While such a commitment requires extra effort, this teacher described how the students always light up when she takes an interest in their lives and how powerful this is as a foundation for building rapport.

Older business owners or managers often resent the fact that they have to go out of their way to build relationships with young people they would not ordinarily socialize with or relate to outside the workplace. This tends to be the case with managers who have a dualistic approach where work and life outside of work are purposely kept separate. Gen Y, however, have a far less dualistic approach to life. For them, blurring the boundaries of relationships and interests at the workplace and away from it is very important to their sense of belonging.

> "AS A PARENT, YOU WILL GET A LOT FURTHER WITH YOUR CHILD IF YOU SEEK TO UNDERSTAND BEFORE YOU SEEK TO BE UNDERSTOOD."

Although building relationships and showing interest in your staff, children or students ought to be a common-sense process, I do work with many people in positions of leadership who struggle to do this in an effective and non-threatening way. If you find yourself in this position, perhaps the ideas below will help you get started:

- **Create space and an environment where conversations can start and develop naturally.** Similar to the way my alma mater used *Dancing with the Staff*, how can your organization foster events and experiences that give space and time for conversations and relationships to build? One business I worked with recently had gone a long way to achieving this in their bi-weekly staff meetings. For the last 12 months, they have started off each meeting with an ongoing darts match. The managers described how, even though this only takes ten minutes each meeting, it goes a long way to creating an atmosphere where people start conversations that lead to topics of shared interest. Other companies have reported that offsite activity days and fun events like pancake lunches work wonders for the level of connection and rapport within a team. If you are an employer, these kinds of initiatives can be significant in that they allow your team to see you outside the role of manager.

- **Develop a *genuine* interest**. Time and time again I speak with parents who have heard about Twitter and Facebook but talk to other parents in order to find out what these sites are all about. Often the response of the other parents is that, although they don't know what the sites are either, they certainly 'don't think they are a good thing'. I ask parents who have done this if they ever considered actually sitting down with their son or daughter and genuinely asking *them* what Facebook and Twitter are. You would be amazed the difference that showing a genuine interest in the technology and world of your son or daughter will make. I am not talking about the sort of interest where you seek out information in order to offer your opinion or judgement. Rather, I am talking about asking the question with no strings attached. As a parent, you will get a lot further with your child if you seek to *understand* before you seek to be *understood*.

- **Leverage events of shared experience**. Everyday there are events and circumstances that occur at a societal level that represent opportunities for starting a conversation. Whether it was the violent storm over the weekend, the final episode of a long-running TV series, or a tragedy in the news, try not to be in such a rush to get on with the day-to-day business of life that you fail to pause and use these experiences as an opportunity to build rapport. Events that lead to a sense of shared experience are a gift to those keen to develop relationships across the generational divide.

- **Engage in two-way conversation**. In your effort to take an interest in the lives of the young people you interact with on a daily basis, be careful not to come across as insincere or forceful in asking questions. Remember that relationships are two-way and young people will develop a natural interest in your life and background as you show one in theirs. A reluctance or hesitation to give or share anything of yourself will create suspicion with this group as your interest will come across as inauthentic.

- **Be proactive in research**. If you discover things about the young people you are working with and take the proactive step to educate yourself about the things that interest them, it will speak volumes. Probably the best example of this I have come across in my travels was the senior school teacher who had made the commitment years ago to make sure she read the free local community newspaper each week to find out how her students' sporting teams had gone the week before so she could ask them about it specifically in class.

- **Diarize points for follow-up**. Life is busy and all too often we forget names, dates and details within minutes of a conversation. One employer I spoke with at a conference had recognized the importance of showing an interest in her younger staff's lives and developed a system to ensure that she remembered the things they talked about. Her system consisted of simply scheduling reminders in her cell phone of dates and events that her staff had mentioned so that she could follow these up. Whether it was the wedding of a sister, family visiting from overseas or something as simple as a birthday, she described the power of remembering and following up on conversations she had with her younger staff. Over the space of just a few months, she noticed a significant difference in the level of rapport and connection she had with them.

I can understand if all this talk of building relationships seems like just too much effort. After all, if you are already run off your feet as a manager, a teacher or a parent, you may wonder when you will possibly find the time or energy to build the level of rapport I am describing here. While building relationships does take time and commitment, I cannot stress strongly enough the critical importance of doing so if you are hoping to engage Generation Y.

Relationships are the foundation for engagement with this group. Once you have a strong relationship, you can do almost everything else wrong and you will still get by with Gen Y. However, without a sense of rapport and relationship, you can use every other strategy we will cover in the following chapters and yet still find engagement to be elusive and difficult to achieve. Sure, building relationships requires an investment of time and energy, but I can assure you that the return on your investment with this group will make it worth your while.

10
CHAPTER TEN
USE MATRIX LEARNING
(T)

This second rule for engaging Generation Y is one geared primarily toward teachers and educators. In case you are unfamiliar with the term 'matrix learning', it is an approach to teaching that focuses on placing *context* around *content*. Put more simply, matrix learning aims to highlight the relevance and connectedness of learning, whether it be in the classroom, at home or even at work.

When the Boomers were at school, education and the process of learning tended to be linear. As mentioned in the previous section, learning for this group was largely considered to be the accumulation and memorising of facts that were to be regurgitated in order to gain a pass. The emphasis was on learning content set out in the curriculum. Questioning, challenging and thinking laterally were generally not accepted and certainly not encouraged.

In past years, subjects and disciplines were islands. They didn't necessarily connect with each other or with the real world. Learning information for the sake of knowing the correct answer was often seen as sufficient.

In that era, a teacher had done their job successfully if the students could correctly answer the question 'what do you *remember* from last week's lesson?' Today, of course, a teacher's success is measured more by a student's response to the question 'What did you *learn* from last week's lesson?'

Having grown up with the World Wide Web, Generation Y will question the relevance and validity of information that isn't dynamically interconnected. With this in mind, Graeme Codrington gives us a good example of what matrix learning might look like.

He describes a process in which students are given an assignment on dolphins. In the course of this assignment they would do research in Biology and then take that research over to Maths for statistical analysis. They use this analysis to form the basis of a formal report which they write in English before finally translating it into French.[98]

The most significant element of this model is that while every subject fulfils its assessment requirements, the student actually understands the purpose and relevance of the learning. In other words, they get a sense of where it fits in and why it is valuable.

While this sort of cross-discipline collaboration may prove challenging practically, it does represent a teaching model and approach to education that is likely to become more of a reality in the coming decades.

Such a methodology need not only apply at a school-wide level – it can also be applied to individual subjects and units of work. The challenge for teachers is to show how the content they are teaching is relevant and connected to the world beyond the classroom.

As we discussed in the previous section, Gen Y tend to ask one question more than any other – 'why?' Not content simply to learn what the curriculum stipulates as worthwhile knowledge, this generation want to understand what the relevance of learning is and how it fits in with everything else they know. They want to know why they need to learn what they are being taught and how it is going to be relevant to their 'real world' lives after school.

It is important to re-emphasize the fact that when this generation ask 'why', it is not necessarily a belligerent, rhetorical challenge to your authority as teacher or parent. Rather, it is a genuine question of relevance that warrants a considered and thoughtful response.

Realising the value of matrix learning and the importance of showing the connections and 'why' of the content, one teacher I spoke to successfully employed this approach to teach his Maths class the concept of ratios. He described how he had one group of students who just didn't get it. No matter how hard he tried, the whole idea of ratios

"GENERATION Y WILL QUESTION THE RELEVANCE AND VALIDITY OF INFORMATION THAT ISN'T DYNAMICALLY INTERCONNECTED."

seemed to be beyond them. At his wit's end, he decided to try a new approach. In a bold move, he took his class on a field trip to the local horse racing track. The class sat there for some time observing emotions ranging from ecstasy to bitter disappointment as thousands of dollars were won and lost in the high-roller's room due to ratios. He described the moments of realization as, one by one, the students understood ratios, not because of a theoretical framework, but because they could see how ratios worked and why they were relevant in real life. As this teacher described it, the class grasped more in that hour at the races than they had in three weeks of classroom learning.

Unorthodox? Absolutely. Effective? You bet!

When it's all boiled down, if learning outcomes are the goal, then teaching with a focus on context, relevance and connectedness is going to be your most effective approach with Gen Y.

It doesn't necessarily require daring excursions or advanced skills in technology – all you need is a bit of creativity and a willingness to try something new.

Sometimes borrowing examples from students' own experiences, technology and popular culture can work most powerfully.

One example I came across of this approach in action involved a music teacher whose greatest challenge was to teach students how to read simple scores and play them on the keyboard. Having tried everything she knew, yet constantly meeting opposition and disinterest from the class, she decided to try a new approach – she charted a ring tone from one of the student's phones.

Bingo! As soon as the music was something the students could relate to, recognize and understand, their ears pricked up and they approached the task with a new interest. Why? Because it suddenly made sense to them.

To see just how effective and powerful this approach can be imagine this: you have been given the task of teaching an appreciation of Shakespeare to a class of 8th grade boys! Seem impossible? That was the challenge facing an English teacher I met recently at a conference.

More accustomed to working with senior classes, this highly experienced teacher dreaded the thought of having to teach a much younger group of boys. 'How am I *ever* going to make Shakespeare relevant and interesting to this class?' she asked herself.

Her choice of *Macbeth* as the text was a good start. Its themes of murder, deceit and violence made it a safe bet content-wise for 15-year-old boys. Her next strategy was to give the students the task of translating large sections of the play into modern-day language.

Following this she asked them to select a scene and re-write it for the screen including all the special effects that would be required to shoot that scene for a movie.

Finally, she asked the students to write scenes from the play in their own language – text dialect. The students abbreviated, cut down and simplified the language to the point where they could send it via text message to each other.

One day, as the class was working on this last step of the project, an amazing thing happened: one of the boys actually looked back at the original Shakespearean language and remarked that he actually liked it better than the text he had just messaged to his friend. As a class they discussed this idea and the majority agreed that Shakespeare's use of language was infinitely more powerful and effective than their own versions of the same text.

Who would have imagined that a class of 8th grade boys would ever come to this conclusion on their own? What an incredible learning outcome! How ironic that asking students to text *Macbeth* to each other would inspire a love for Shakespeare.

This is the power of making content connect with something that is relevant.

Looking outside the school

A teacher's ability to show how information is relevant to a student's future is a powerful way of engaging them in the learning process. One excellent strategy is to bring in workplace 'experts' to speak to students. Many teachers would be surprised how willing and interested business people are to visit schools to address students about what they do. With some deliberate prompting, many of these visitors will be more than capable of making the connection between what you are teaching your students and what they do on a daily basis in business. In a sense, these visiting experts become your advocate.

It often doesn't matter how many times you tell the students that what they are learning is relevant – after all, what else would you be expected to say? However, watch how quickly and easily your students will listen to and believe someone from the outside who says exactly the same thing!

11

CHAPTER ELEVEN
CHAPTER ELEVEN
FOCUS ON OUTCOMES OVER PROCESS

This next key to engaging Gen Y relates to the way in which you measure performance and output. Focussing on outcomes over process is about clarifying and prioritising the reason *why* you do what you do (the outcomes) as opposed to *what* you do to achieve it (the process).

Gen Y are highly outcomes-driven. Red tape, bureaucracy and unnecessary structure are all huge turn-offs to a postmodern, impatient and pragmatic generation. The challenge, however, is that the Builders, and to a lesser extent Boomers, are often so attached to the processes that guide and guard their organizational cultures that they lose sight of the outcomes they set out to achieve in the first place.

It is easy to see where such an attitude originates. After all, Builders, in particular, were so heavily influenced by the industrial revolution and both World Wars that they tend to see organizations as only operating effectively when they are mechanical, military-like and highly structured. For this group, the role of the individual was to be a small cog in a large wheel in an even larger machine. Builders knew their place on the production line of the workplace and performed their roles with due diligence, regardless of whether they knew where their contribution fitted into the broader scheme of things or not.

Even though many Builders are now retired and have handed the reins of their organizations and institutions over to Boomers, the legacy of their organizational paradigm is still evident. Whether in the private or public sector, many of the institutions that form the foundation of our modern society have cultures and a momentum that were set by the Builders. Predictability, measurability and bureaucracy tend to define the organizations that Builders created. In a modern climate, however, these very characteristics tend to conflict with the core work and life values of Generation Y – flexibility, collaboration, teamwork and innovation.

Many educators and public servants I work with express frustration with the bureaucracy that seems to work against the strategies they are attempting to implement in an effort to increase their engagement with young people.

"PREDICTABILITY, MEASURABILITY AND BUREAUCRACY TEND TO DEFINE THE ORGANIZATIONS THAT BUILDERS CREATED."

The challenge for the Boomer and, increasingly, Gen X leaders now at the helm of these institutions is to re-evaluate historical processes and structure in light of modern-day outcomes and needs. A failure to do so will create enormous obstacles in attracting, motivating and engaging Gen Y.

Looking outside the corporate and business arena, the focus on process over outcomes can also be seen in many households and schools. Institutions, be they family, faith-based or educational, can so easily slip into the trap of becoming process-driven rather than outcomes-driven. In such organizations, the focus tends to be on repeating how things have been done previously to ensure that the successes of yesterday are repeated tomorrow. Such an approach ignores the reality that the way things have been done in the past may no longer be as relevant, appropriate or competitive.

This trap is an easy one to fall into and it tends to happen by degrees over long periods of time. Often it is not until a new paradigm or way of operating challenges our much-loved processes and organizational 'sacred cows' that we recognize their existence and our allegiance to them.

3 SYMPTOMS OF PROCESS-DRIVEN INSTITUTIONS

A) They are inflexible

If I had to choose just one characteristic that describes the type of organization that attracts and engages Generation Y, it would have to be *flexibility*. This generation loves to work for organizations that are organic, loosely structured and responsive to change and diversity. The only problem is that flexibility is often the first casualty of process-driven institutions. In their drive to measure performance and benchmark results, such organizations tend to diminish the role and value of the individual.

While structure is necessary in any organization, developing processes and cultures that can be flexible and adaptive is critical if you want to attract Gen Y.

There are a number of areas in which flexibility will go a long way to engaging Gen Y staff. However, for our purposes here I want to touch on just three – dress codes, work hours and work location.

- **Dress codes**. Generation Y love to work for companies that allow them to express their individuality in an appropriate manner. One of the most powerful ways this group does so is through their attire. As I mentioned in section two, younger generations tend to view work and life in a less dualistic way than their forebears. In other words, it is better for Gen Y if the line between work and life outside of work is blurry.

Probably the best example of an organization that understands the importance of relaxed dress codes is the global telecommunications company, Vodafone. Having presented to Vodafone's executive team on a number of occasions, I have been able to get an insight into the deliberate steps this organization has put in place to develop a relaxed yet professional corporate culture. Vodafone's policy on dress codes is to dress neatly and casually unless you are meeting with clients. This is an approach that resonates well with Gen Y and Vodafone's engagement figures reflect it.

- **Work hours**. What if you were to find that your Gen Y staff perform best between the hours of 11.30 am and 7.30 pm? Assuming they are in a role that would not be affected by working hours such as these, would you let your staff keep these hours, or demand that they work the same hours as you and everyone else in the office? A process-driven organization would likely go with the latter. Standardization and consistency are the name of the game.

Furthermore, what if you have staff members who have completed their days work in six hours? Would you allow and even encourage them to go home once they are finished or is it more important that they stay at their desk till the stroke of 5.00 pm 'because everybody else has to'? To pose the question differently, are you rewarding staff for performing or for playing the game?

- **Work location**. If your staff could do their job from home wearing their pajamas just as easily as from the office, would you still measure their commitment using the 'butts-on-seats' approach or would you look more at what they produce and the quality of their work? Impractical, you say? Consider the example cited by Don Tapscott of US electrical goods retailer Best Buy. In an effort to make their workplace more appealing to younger workers, Best Buy have implemented a program called ROWE (Results-Only Work Environment) which allows corporate employees to do their work at anytime anywhere as long as they get the work done. As of June 2008, 80% of Best Buy's corporate staff were participating in the ROWE program and the company now plans on expanding the programs to their stores – a first for any retailer.[99]

Indicating a broader trend, American health insurance giant Aetna recently implemented a work-from-home or telework program in an effort to retain talented employees. Since its inception, the program has grown exponentially to the point where 27% of the Aetna's workforce now work from home. Other companies who have developed work-from-home programs include American Airlines, TDS Telecom, Sprint and Xerox.[100]

As jobs become less workplace-specific due to advances in communication technology and the advent of telecommuting, more and more work can be done in a location other than the office. What's more, it's a win/win for both employees and employers. Author of *Microtrends* Mark Penn sites research indicating that stay-at-home workers actually log *more* hours than their counterparts in offices yet still report far higher rates of job satisfaction.[101]

More often than not, however, it is organizational cultures, policies and processes, rather than commercial factors, which prevent employees and managers from taking advantage of these trends.

B) Process-driven institutions separate reward from output

I recently spoke with a friend who was on the verge of resigning from a call center job he had previously described as lucrative and enjoyable. When I asked him why he was leaving the company, I was surprised to hear his response.

He described to me how each Monday for the last three months he had been summoned into the manager's office only to be chastised for his failure to reach outbound call quotas in the week before. The irony was that even though my friend had not come close to achieving his call quotas, his sales figures outstripped

> "PROCESS IS NOT THE ENEMY BUT YOUR PROCESSES MUST CONNECT WITH, AND BE SUBSERVIENT TO, YOUR OUTCOMES."

each of his workmates by at least two-to-one. And yet, despite his protests and the results he pointed to, my friend's manager saw nothing but the failure to comply with the process by which he measured performance – namely call quotas.

At the time of writing, my friend had resigned from this company. While it is a great shame that he was treated in this way and left the company as a result, it is an even greater shame that organizational cultures and practices such as these are more common than many realize. Countless organizations and institutions separate output from reward and become so focused on the processes and benchmarks of performance that they lose sight of the reason the benchmarks were put there in the first place. Process in itself is not the enemy but your processes must connect with and be subservient to your outcomes if you have any hope of attracting and retaining Gen Y staff.

In education, separation of reward from output will also have adverse effects on engaging Gen Y. Much of our system of education tends to focus more on learning as a time-dependant rite of passage than as a recognition of growth and development. In other words, students who perform well and excel are often held back until it is their time or turn to progress. However, at the same time, students who don't perform well through lack of effort or ability are often automatically progressed without the necessary skills and capabilities.

I think this is perhaps why competency-based training works so well with a pragmatic group such as Gen Y. For those who are unfamiliar with the concept, competency-based training is an approach to education that focuses on what students can *do* with what they know. Progress within a competency-based training program is not based on time but rather on ability. As soon as students have achieved or demonstrated the outcomes required in a module, they can move on.

Competency-based training is effective with Gen Y for two reasons. Firstly, it shows the connection between what the student is learning and an outcome that can be measured and demonstrated in a tangible way – it answers the 'why' question. Secondly, it allows a student's learning to be self-paced – as soon as they have achieved or demonstrated the outcomes required in a module, students are rewarded and can progress regardless of where their peers are up to.

Of course competency-based training will not necessarily work across all disciplines and subject areas. Although traditionally used in vocational colleges, more and more schools at a secondary and tertiary level are adopting the philosophy, and even the structure, of competency-based training. I suspect we will see a movement toward this in the coming years as education continues to become more individualized and performance-driven. Such a trend goes to the heart of a long-standing philosophical debate within educational circles – should students be expected to fit educational institutions or should educational institutions fit the needs of students.

C) Process-driven institutions are rules-focused

If process guards and guides the way organizations operate, then rules are the method by which processes are reinforced and sustained. It is therefore impossible to truly understand what it means to shift from being process-driven to outcomes-driven without a discussion of the very nature of rules and how they shape our attitudes and behavior.

Consider this: the very moment you find yourself upset, hurt or angry with the things or people around you, your emotional response indicates little more than that one of your personal rules or expectations has been violated.

It's true isn't it? Whether in relationships, at work or on the highway, we all approach life with sets of rules that dictate the circumstances under which we feel we can be happy, content and satisfied. Often, these rules are so subconscious and implicit that we are unaware of their existence until someone or something dares to break them. Many teachers walk into the school each day with an often unexpressed set of rules about how the classroom should look and sound, and how the students ought to act and respond, only to wonder why they get so upset when rules and expectations on their 'checklist' are not met.

The simple reality is, each of us is far more responsible for the irritation, anger and hurt we feel than those around us who we accuse and blame so vehemently. The more rules we place around how life, people and events ought to be, the more ways we create for ourselves to feel disappointment, frustration and upset. This is, of course, easy to say and far harder to do. And yet, that doesn't make it any less true. Further still, it is as true at an organizational level as it is at an interpersonal level.

Blame and responsibility aside, the point to consider is this: how many of the rules and expectations you place on your children, employees and students are really worth the friction, arguments and pain they cause? Furthermore, how many of these rules and expectations are linked to an outcome and how many are simply there as tools for reinforcing process?

This question seems to hit home most with parents. There isn't a week that goes by that I don't hear a parent express disappointment, irritation or frustration with the behavior and choices of a son or daughter. When I ask what exactly has led to such an impasse in the relationship I am often astonished at how trivial the causal factors seem to be. I'm not saying that the things which lead to tension between yourself and the younger generation don't *feel* significant in the moment, I just wonder how important those things really are.

Perhaps it would be worth applying the 20-year test to some of the rules to which you demand and expect compliance. In other words, will the present argument, altercation or breach of behavior even matter in 20 years' time? Furthermore, what are the chances that you will be able to remember it that far down the track? How much will non-compliance with this particular rule or expectation even matter when it is viewed with the non-emotional clarity of hindsight? So often it is the small and insignificant things that cause the most friction in relationships. As bestselling American author Francis Frangipane suggests: *People don't usually stumble over boulders: they stumble over stones – relatively small things.*[102]

Sometimes getting perspective is the most effective way to determine the rules and expectations that are worth enforcing. I love the story American baseball legend Harmon Killebrew tells about when his father used to play with him and his brother in the backyard. In response to his mother's protest of, 'You're tearing up the grass', Harmon's father would respond, 'We're not raising grass, we're raising boys.'

Parents – whether it is the age-old generational war over clean bedrooms, towels hung neatly on the rail, or tidy haircuts – can I encourage you to pick your battles carefully if you want to move toward a position of engaging Generation Y? Of course some boundaries are worth enforcing and some battles are necessary to fight. When it comes to personal safety and significant life choices, there will be times when you

"SMART ORGANIZATIONS ARE BEGINNING TO SEE THE 'WHY' QUESTION AS A GIFT RATHER THAN AN AFFRONT TO AUTHORITY AND THE STATUS QUO."

need to 'put your foot down'. However, just like the boy who cried wolf, you may have eroded your credibility and authority to enforce these important boundaries if you have consistently overreacted to every small and insignificant misdemeanor along the way.

In considering the perspective that hindsight brings to the rules that many of us live by, I was reminded of an email I received a number of years ago. This email included an excerpt from a letter published in *The Chicago Tribune* in January 1980. Entitled 'If I Had My Life to Live Over Again', this letter was penned by celebrated US humorist Erma Bombeck. It read:

Someone asked me the other day what I would change if I had my life to live over again. My automatic response was, of course, 'nothing'. But then I thought about it and changed my mind. The truth is, if had my life to live again, I would have done many things differently.

I would never have insisted the car windows be rolled up on a summer day because my hair had just been sprayed. I would have invited friends over to dinner even if the carpet was stained and the sofa faded. I would have eaten popcorn in the living room and worried less about the dirt when I lit the fireplace. I would have burnt the pink candle sculptured like a rose before it melted while being stored.

I would have sat cross-legged on the lawn with my children and never worried about the grass stains. I would have cried and laughed less when watching TV and more while watching real life. I would have eaten less cottage cheese and more ice-cream. I would have never bought anything just because it was practical, wouldn't show marks, or was guaranteed to last a lifetime. When one of my children kissed me impetuously, I would never have said 'later – now go get washed up for dinner.'

There would be fewer rules, more I love you's, more I'm sorry's and more I'm listening. But mostly, given another shot at life, I would seize every minute of it and not give that minute back until there was nothing left.

An interesting perspective, isn't it?

Parents, please think twice next time you are tempted to fly off the handle in reaction to the small (or even large) things that your children do that irritate, disappoint or upset you. Can I also give you the same challenge if you are an employer or teacher of this group. I urge you to be humble and honest enough to ask yourself if it is possible that your frustrations with Gen Y are more a result of your own process-driven rules and expectations than the specific actions, decisions and attitudes of this group that you may point to. Furthermore, give the infringement or non-compliant behavior the 20-year test. You may well find that avoiding arguments, debates and shouting matches creates the environment in which an engaging relationship can truly flourish.

As we have already discussed, the question of 'why' is one that defines Generation Y. It is important to note, however, that nothing will cause this group to ask 'why' more frequently than process that seems disconnected from outcomes.

Smart organizations are beginning to see the 'why' question as a *gift* rather than an affront to authority and the status quo. As long as this question is asked in a tone that is constructive, the question 'why' from this younger generation may well be the greatest source of innovation and creativity that your organization has. After all, this group will look at the processes in place and ask why you do things the way you do. As evidenced by a recent survey where 75% of Gen Ys reported that they would like to find new ways of accomplishing their jobs, Don Tapscott suggests that this is a generation who are 'bent on being innovative in the office.'[103]

With the benefit of fresh eyes and an implicit understanding of the capabilities and potential of technology, your Gen Y employees and team members will be able to see possibilities and new ways of achieving outcomes that you may never have thought of. These new processes may well save you time, make you money and even give you a competitive edge!

Managers and leaders, be careful not to simply dismiss the question of 'why' from your young team members. Contrary to popular opinion, they are not simply trying to rile against the system or challenge the established rules for the sake of doing so. They are genuinely looking for an answer to the question of 'why' and will happily comply with expectations, rules, protocols and procedures once they understand the purpose behind them. On the other hand, the most counterproductive response to the 'why' question is always going to be 'because that's just the way we've always done it'.

Ultimately, choosing to focus on outcomes rather than process comes back to communicating what the outcome or end result is to your young people and then giving them flexibility, empowerment and permission to find their own way of achieving it. Being outcomes-driven is about projecting a clear vision of an exciting possibility. It is about saying 'this is where we want to get to and what we want to achieve. *How* we get there is not as important as making sure that we do.'

By all means, give this younger generation boundaries, tell them the stories of what has worked in the past, offer to mentor them, but above all else, give them space. Organizations and institutions that find ways of doing this effectively stand the best chance of not only engaging Gen Y, but also staying relevant and competitive in our modern age.

12

CHAPTER TWELVE
ADOPT A
FACILITATOR ROLE

(E) (T) (P)

If you trace the origins of our current systems of education and training back through history, you find yourself in a time when the responsibility for distributing information and knowledge was held almost exclusively by the Church. During the Dark Ages clergy were charged with the duty of imparting information, knowledge and truth to the uneducated masses. To be a 'teacher' meant that you were the source or fountain of knowledge.

Over time, this task was gradually relegated to academics. Professors and learned men shared the responsibility of gathering, evaluating and imparting knowledge. You can still see evidence today of the old links between academia and the Church – at a university graduation day the vice-chancellor still wears formal gowns not dissimilar to those worn by a bishop or priest.

From those early origins through to today's organized systems of education, we see one common thread – the role of teacher as the source or fountain of knowledge. To be fair, this approach was both appropriate and necessary in past times. After all, books were valuable and rare, information was held by those in power and access to education was reserved for the aristocracy.

These days, however, the Information Age has profoundly changed the nature and needs of young people. Consider this: a teenager today with access to the internet has more information at their fingertips than entire countries did just 50 years ago. Students are more travelled, 'worldly-wise' and informed than ever before. Just two words typed into a Google search can return well over 100,000 articles in 0.37 of a second.

All this means one thing – teachers as the source of knowledge are becoming increasingly unnecessary.

The institutions and organizations that are successfully engaging today's young people recognize this shift. Nowadays, educators, parents and managers must turn their focus from being fountains of knowledge to being facilitators of learning.

While the modern era has afforded society unprecedented levels of education and access to knowledge, it has also brought with it new challenges. The paradox today is that information and knowledge don't necessarily go hand in hand. They are not even directly related. In other words, the fact that we have more information at our disposal does not automatically mean that we are more knowledgeable. Some would even argue that our current information overload has resulted in us actually knowing less than ever before.

In an information-rich age the challenge is to sift through the relative sea of information and create retained knowledge that is, as we discussed in Chapter 10, both relevant and connected. This is where a good facilitator comes in.

THREE SKILLS OF A GOOD FACILITATOR

A Good facilitators are 'master-askers'

Facilitating learning requires a different mentality and range of skills to that of being a fountain of knowledge. It means shifting from a focus on knowing the right *answers* to asking the right *questions*.

For a generation who will enter a constantly changing workforce, a commitment to lifelong learning and upskilling will be a necessity. Good facilitators arm young people with arguably the most important skill they will need – the skill of learning how to learn.

I find that parents are far better facilitators of learning when their children are younger but tend to lose this skill as adolescence sets in. I remember as a young child asking my mom how to spell certain words. Even though she knew how to spell the word in question and she knew that I knew that she knew, her response would always be the same: 'Look it up for yourself in the dictionary.'

This response used to frustrate me enormously because all I wanted was the answer. Mom, however, in her wisdom knew that knowing the answer was less important than my knowing how to find the answer myself. As she would say: 'What if I'm not around next time

> "A TEENAGER TODAY WITH ACCESS TO THE INTERNET HAS MORE INFORMATION AT THEIR FINGERTIPS THAN ENTIRE COUNTRIES DID JUST FIFTY YEARS AGO."

you need to know how to spell a different word? I want you to know how to figure it out on your own.'

Most parents can identify with this approach – you may even have subjected your child to the same torture when they were younger.

However, as I work with groups of parents who are trying to help their teenage children choose career pathways and subjects at school, the role of facilitating and asking questions seems to be very low on the list of parental priorities.

Parents want to know the answers. This is always made especially clear to me when I speak to parent groups about how to prepare their children for the changing workforce. During one of my seminars on this topic called *Equipping Today's Students for Tomorrow*, audience members seem desperate to write down every statistic I mention regarding skills shortages, growth industries and employment trends in the hope of not missing a thing.

Following such a session I will often be inundated with fraught parents wanting me to tell them what career advice they should give their son or daughter when they get home. My response is almost always the same: 'Don't give answers or advice. Ask *questions*.' Ask them what they like. Ask them what they are good at. Ask them what they already know. Ask if they are aware of the websites that will help them find the information for themselves.

That said, while questions are a powerful strategy for engaging young people, it is often *how* you ask a question that will determine its effectiveness.

Well-asked questions are powerful. Recognizing this to be true, Albert Einstein once famously claimed: *If I had an hour to solve a problem and my life depended on the solution, I would spend the first 55 minutes determining the proper question to ask, for once I knew the proper question, I could solve the problem in less than five minutes.*

To better understand what constitutes a 'good' question, I interviewed an award-winning counselor and social worker with over 30 years experience. Drawing on countless hours of asking powerful and strategic questions of her clients, this counselor suggested a number of keys to asking effective questions. I believe that many of these will work as well for you at home, in the classroom, or in the workplace as they do in a counselor's office:

i   **Avoid closed questions** that lead to a yes or no response. View questions as an opportunity to open discussion and encourage thought rather than simply a test or challenge designed to a get the correct response. In their book *The Art of Powerful Questions* Vogt, Brown and Isaacs state: *Questions open the door to dialogue and discovery. They are an invitation to creativity and breakthrough thinking.*[104]

ii   **Start questions well** with words like *who? what? when? where?* or *how?* rather than *why?* Questions that begin with 'why?' tend to prompt a defensive or adversarial response – ask *'What made you do that?'* rather than *'Why did you do that?'*

iii   **Ask one question at a time** and keep questions short and sharp. If young people are unsure of what you are asking them they won't respond for fear of looking stupid.

iv   **Never ask loaded or leading questions** that imply a prejudice e.g. *'Do you listen to deafening music like all young people?'*

v   **Ask questions with an enquiring, curious and interested tone.** Questions that interrogate, embarrass or have the goal of 'catching out' the respondent will destroy vital rapport and trust e.g. *'When are you going to take charge of your life and look for a job?'* Using phrases like *'Tell me about that'*, *'What do you mean?'*, *'Can you elaborate for me?'* gives the respondent permission to think and learn out loud. Well-asked questions have the unique potential to bring underlying assumptions to the surface and lead to self-reflection.

vi **Never ridicule or dismiss a response.** An incorrect or misguided answer is simply an opportunity to ask another question. It is crucial that respondents feel safe to suggest an opinion or have a go.

vii **Answer a question with a question.** If your child or student asks you a question that is designed to catch you out or to test you, respond with a question of your own. It's no wonder that many parents and teachers describe their homes and

> "IT IS OFTEN HOW YOU ASK A QUESTION THAT WILL DETERMINE ITS EFFECTIVENESS."

classrooms as 'out of control'. After all, the first lesson any salesperson learns when going out in the field is that whoever is asking the questions is in control of the conversation. If your students or children are asking all the questions and you are giving all the answers, it is easy to see who is controlling (let's call it 'leading') the conversation. The challenge is to respond to their questions with questions of your own that are not patronizing, trite or insincere.

viii **Be genuine.** If you are not interested in the response, don't ask the question.

ix **Recognize that all questions have an impact** regardless of the response. Sometimes the best questions will be dismissed immediately by the respondent only to prompt thought and consideration after the fact.

x   **Reduce your expectations** of what constitutes a 'good response'. Sometimes a grunt is an answer. Be grateful for that and respond positively and respectfully.

Questions are indeed the answer. Regardless of whether you are an employer, a parent or a teacher, questions are the key to unlocking your young people's creativity, imagination, and capacity to reason. If you can get good at asking questions, you are more than halfway there.

Another questioning technique I have come across, called restorative questioning, is being used effectively in engaging students with problematic and anti-social behaviors. The basic premise of restorative questioning is that human beings are happier, more cooperative, more productive and more likely to make positive choices if those in authority adopt a position of doing *with* as opposed to doing *to* or doing *for*. It is an empowering process of asking questions that provides the opportunity for students to share their feelings, build relationships and problem-solve, and when there is wrongdoing, to play an active role in addressing the wrong and making things right.[105] As such, it is less about 'getting to the bottom of things' or assigning blame and responsibility and more about developing dialogue and understanding.

Some examples of restorative questioning include:

- What happened?

- What were you thinking at the time?

- What have you thought about it since?

- Who has been affected by what you've done? In what way?

- What do you think you need to do to make things right?

B) Good facilitators give space for self-directed learning

In 2006 I spent a number of months helping implement a government funded community mentoring program in a disadvantaged area of Sydney.

The program was unique in its approach as it gave community volunteers the opportunity to coach a young person while they themselves received personal coaching and mentoring. We had a range of community volunteers involved – business owners, church leaders, teachers and retirees.

It was interesting to watch the program develop and to see how the different volunteer mentors settled into their new role. The business owners, familiar with the idea of professional training, seemed to hit the ground running. Likewise, the church leaders who were used to pastoral support roles took to mentoring like ducks to water.

In stark contrast, the teachers really struggled. They seemed to have enormous trouble adopting the skill set of a mentor. The feedback from young people across the program was that the teachers were using their mentoring sessions as teaching opportunities. They spent the whole session giving advice, talking far more than they listened and sometimes, even setting homework for their protégés!

The challenge for me and others involved was to help these teachers recognize that this approach to mentoring was both counter-productive and inappropriate. It took many weeks and a number of difficult conversations to help them see that there were alternative approaches. Essentially, we had to train teachers in the skill of facilitation. We found that one of the hardest things for these teachers was to be comfortable with two things – silence and ambiguity.

The strength and value of coaching and mentoring in personal development is that it focuses on self-directed learning. We found that once these teachers had a clear set of the right questions they could ask their protégé, the next challenge was encouraging the teachers to ask the question and then to be silent. And then... be silent some more. Now they were stepping into uncomfortable territory.

For these teachers, while it was a steep learning curve, it was one worth undertaking. What they learned was that silence is the key to giving a young person space to connect some of the dots for themselves.

Over time our teacher-mentors began to describe how liberating they found the whole idea of facilitating. They no longer felt a sense of responsibility for every learning outcome in a mentoring session. They told of the elation and satisfaction they felt when a student had a 'light-bulb moment' not because of something that they as 'teacher' had said, but because of something the student had realized on their own.

Transferring this concept to the classroom, the home or the workplace depends on how comfortable you feel with leaving the necessary space and silence that will allow self-directed learning to take place. Do you pose a question then feel so uncomfortable in the resulting gap that you jump in and answer the question yourself?

In a similar vein, do you feel the need to have every unit of work neatly tied up by the end of the conversation or lesson?

Giving students space and time to come to their own conclusions and to develop their own ideas is a vital step in the facilitation of learning. For a postmodern generation, answers that are readily given will tend to be dismissed as superficial, simple or naïve. Questions that linger and allow for ambiguity and complexity will connect powerfully with Gen Y.

C) **Good facilitators clarify what has been learnt**

One of the most significant elements of the modern pedagogical (teaching) models being implemented in schools and colleges around the world is an emphasis on making the implicit explicit. In other words, how can you show young people what they have already learnt or what they currently know?

In *Nexgen's* work helping students prepare for job interviews in schools, I have constantly been amazed by how many young people underestimate themselves and their skills. Time after time students maintain that they haven't got any skills to offer a potential employer simply because they have never had a job.

While I understand what they mean when they say this, it points to a greater problem with many young people's perception of themselves – they don't know what they know. Once I reframe the question along the lines of: *Have you ever done group work?* or *Have your teachers ever had you do a presentation in front of the class?* then the students start to get the point. Young people have a whole range of skills – it is just that they don't recognize them.

A good facilitator helps students retrace their steps. They point out what has been learnt and explain why that learning is valuable. The role of making the implicit explicit is powerful because it helps students see progress and development. Many times students feel overwhelmed by the learning process. Getting a sense of growth and achievement is key to keeping students motivated and engaged in education as it attaches a quantifiable value to learning.

13

CHAPTER THIRTEEN
GIVE REGULAR POSITIVE FEEDBACK

(E) (T)

Recognition. It is that all-powerful motivator that babies will cry for, grown men will die for... and Gen Y will work for.

If you want to tap into young people's motivation and creativity then encouragement and affirmation is a fail-safe tool. Highlighting this in a recent article for the *Wall Street Journal,* journalist Jeffrey Zaslow cited a scooter store in Texas which, having recognized the importance of affirmation to Gen Y, now employs a full-time 'celebrations assistant'. The job description for this position includes throwing large amounts of confetti at employees each week, handing out helium balloons and 'randomly showing up at employees desks offering high-fives to acknowledge a job well done'.[106]

Crazy, isn't it? And yet more and more companies are resorting to similar (albeit less strange) extremes to engage their younger staff.

While confetti and balloons may go some way towards showing appreciation and creating a culture of encouragement, can I suggest that there are probably more subtle and powerful ways to give affirmation and recognize achievement?

Recognition of special talents, successfully completed tasks, incremental improvements in performance, new haircuts and punctuality are some of the small things that can make a world of difference.

The reality is that people tend to raise or lower their performance to the levels of expectation set for them. As the great German writer Johann Wolfgang von Goethe said: *If you treat an individual as if he were what he ought to be and could be, he will become what he ought to be and could be.* It goes without saying that expecting and recognizing the best in others is the safest way to ensure that the best is what they give.

A few years ago I came across a wonderful book that highlighted the power of affirmation and encouragement. Written by management guru Ken Blanchard, *Whale Done* explores the process by which whales are trained at SeaWorld.[107]

The fictitious lead character in *Whale Done* is a trainer called Dave. Drawing on his years of experience training whales, Dave highlights powerful principles for leading and creating positive change in people. He contends that the only way to train whales to perform the incredible tricks they do is to make use of positive responses and affirmation. He highlights the significance of identifying positive progress and affirming this progress, no matter how big or small.

In translating these principles to leading people, Ken Blanchard encourages the reader to develop the skill of looking for and 'catching' people doing the right thing (rather than the wrong thing) and then responding well. He lists four essential elements of a positive response:

1. **Praise** people immediately in a sincere and honest way.

2. **Be specific** about what they did right or *almost* right.

3. **Share** your positive feelings about what they did.

4. **Encourage** them to keep up the good work.

Although the principles Ken Blanchard outlines in *Whale Done* are true for managing and inspiring any staff member regardless of age, I would suggest that using tools of affirmation and recognition are perhaps most important for those working with Gen Y. Why? Because rightly or wrongly, encouragement and affirmation is the only language this group knows as highlighted in previous sections. Criticism will tend to fall on deaf ears for a generation who have only ever been praised.

I would add four other keys to the above list when it comes to recognizing and affirming your Gen Y students, staff and children:

- **Affirm Publically.** While it is true that most Gen Xers shun public recognition and affirmation, Gen Y are the polar opposite. This group love an award, a trophy, a mention in the company bulletin or a photo on the noticeboard even if they pretend they don't. Perhaps the only exception to this rule of thumb is with adolescent boys (and sometimes girls) between the ages of 12-14.

- **Affirm Personally.** For a generation that has grown up surrounded by technology, the impact and importance of the personal touch is so much greater. Prof. Jean Twenge argues that our modern information age has left us relationally malnourished from eating a junk-food diet of instant messages, email and phone calls, at the expense of live, in-person interaction.[108] This is certainly true of the tech-saturated Gen Y.

  Rather than just sending an email of congratulations on a job well done, why not take the extra two minutes to see your Gen Y staff in person. A shake of the hand and a pat on the back can mean the world to a group who are often looking for physical connection. In the same vein, a personally addressed handwritten thank you note or card will go a long way.

- **Affirm Proportionately**. In the first instance, it is important to give praise and affirmation to Gen Y in proportion to the achievement or effort applied. If you make a big deal out of small things, they will often dismiss your encouragement as insincere flattery.

  Along the same lines, it is important to not fall into the trap of over-praising or adopting the "everyone's a winner" approach with this group. Gen Y are not stupid and will quickly grow cynical if each person in a team, class or workplace receives an award regardless of achievement. Tim Elmore argues that such an approach actually robs young people of a genuine pride in their achievements along with motivation to strive for excellence and improvement.[109]

  In a different way, it is important that affirmation is given proportionately to both the person and the performance. A sole focus on praising a young person for what they *do* will condition them to strive for and rely on external feedback and praise for every action or achievement. It also communicates the message that an individual is only valuable for what they can do or produce. This is often what leads people to become performance addicts or chronic people-pleasers later in life.

  Conversely, a young person who only ever receives praise simply for who they *are* regardless of what they do will become conditioned that effort and performance don't matter. Such an attitude tends to foster laziness, a false sense of entitlement and the narcissism described in section one.

- **Affirm Practically**. The more tangible and practical you can make rewards and recognitions, the more motivating they will be for Gen Y. Sure, they love employee of the month awards and efficiency plaques, but sometimes movie tickets, dinner out or a bottle of wine will mean even more.

While I come across very few managers and leaders who are resistant to the idea of making positive affirmation a priority in their work with young people, I am often asked the question of how to respond when constructive criticism or firm coaching is required. In other words, while it is all well and good to develop the habit and culture of giving regular positive affirmation,

> "IF YOU TREAT AN INDIVIDUAL AS IF HE WERE WHAT HE OUGHT TO BE AND COULD BE, HE WILL BECOME WHAT HE OUGHT TO BE AND COULD BE."

what about when those you lead persistently do the wrong thing or show little regard for your efforts to acknowledge their strengths and positive choices? I think this is definitely something worth discussing considering how badly Gen Y can react to any negative feedback.

My hope in this chapter has been in some way to challenge the natural default mode of many managers and organizations that look to catch their people doing the wrong thing and then punish it. However, I believe there is still a place for honest, justified, constructive and well-intentioned negative feedback. The key is to develop the art of giving it in a way that builds rather than breaks down, that strengthens rather than discourages.

Author and management consultant John Reh offers some practical tips for giving negative feedback:[110]

1. **Get your emotions under control**. It is important not to act impulsively and critique someone else's actions when you are angry or upset. When operating from emotion, you may well say something you don't really mean or react unreasonably to something that is said to you.

2. **Find a private place**. It is important not to add insult to injury by embarrassing the person you are speaking to. No one wants to receive negative feedback in front of other people. Sometimes it is unavoidable, but that should be a last resort. Take a meeting in your office, call the person into a meeting room or step into the lunch room if it is vacant.

3. **Focus on the action, not on the person**. You create an immediate barrier when you criticize someone personally. Focus instead on what you want to change. Focus on their performance not their personhood; their actions not their identity.

4. **Be specific**. It is not enough to tell someone that they are doing a bad job. You must identify the specific actions, words or attitudes you want the person to address if they are to truly understand and be able to respond.

5. **Be timely**. Negative feedback should be given as soon as possible after the event. If you see an employee being rude to a customer for instance, don't wait for their annual performance review or until you have tallied up a number of grievances and then ambush them.

6. **Be calm**. Don't become confrontational by raising your voice or adopting a menacing stance. The other person will become defensive and won't hear what you are trying to tell them if you approach the conversation in an aggressive manner.

7. **Reaffirm your faith in the person**. This reinforces step three. It is vital to be clear that you still have faith in them as a person and in their abilities regardless of the action or performance you are addressing. When performing step seven, however, make every effort not to be perceived as patronizing or insincere.

8. **Stop talking**. After you have outlined the specific and recent actions were inappropriate, and why, be sure to give the person an opportunity to respond.

9. **Define positive steps**. Set clear expectations and a plan around what future performance is appropriate for the employee. If there are specific things that either you or the employee need to start doing or need to stop doing, be sure they are clearly identified.

10. **Get over it**. After you have given the negative feedback and agreed on a resolution, move on and don't bear a grudge.

To the above list I would add one very profound but simple principle I learned a few years ago from a wise mentor; *always say the negative and write the positive*. I found this one piece of advice so helpful in relating to others. A negative comment written down can be stewed over and analyzed for days, weeks or even years. In contrast, spoken negative words can seem potent at the time but tend to evaporate quickly and fade from memory.

The key principle here is to prioritize the use of regular positive affirmation if you want to bring out the best in the young people you work with. Imagine the difference it would make if our schools and colleges were filled with teachers who chose to focus on the positive progress and choices students make on a daily basis rather than dwelling on, and thus reinforcing, negative behaviors.

What if our homes were places where angst and arguments brought about by the 'nag-cycle' stopped and, as a result, we saw constructive relationships formed based on encouragement and affirmation?

What about the workplace? Imagine the difference a focus on positive affirmation could make. After all, the things that you recognize and reward in your staff will be the things they repeat.

While I believe that changes like these are possible, I am not suggesting that they are easy to make. They may be *simple* changes but they are by no means *easy*. If, however, you are serious about developing an engaging relationship with your Gen Y employees, students or children, affirmation and encouragement will be a significant step forward in achieving this end.

14

SET SHORT TERM, CHALLENGING GOALS
(E)

When you consider the fast-paced, constantly changing and technology-driven world of sound bites that Generation Y has grown up in, it is no wonder that the yardsticks of performance used in much of the business world are just too long.

Most businesses, for example, make use of performance reviews and dialogues only on an annual basis. These meetings are often the only time for the previous year's achievements to be formally evaluated and the coming year's goals set in place. However, if

"BE CAREFUL NOT TO ASSUME THAT YOU KNOW WHAT YOUR STAFF WANT. THEIR GOALS AND DESIRES MAY BE VERY DIFFERENT TO YOUR OWN."

young people rarely stay in positions for more than two years as is so often the case, annual performance reviews quickly lose their effectiveness as a tool for motivating and stimulating output.

A good number of the organizations that I have presented to and consulted with in recent years are actually shifting the way they conduct performance reviews and are now scheduling these monthly or at least quarterly as opposed to annually. The feedback I have received from these organizations is that more frequent reviews are working because they allow Gen Y to set smaller, short-term goals that are more motivating.

A quick tip on the effective use of performance dialogues also relates to the location and context in which you have them. Try taking these meetings outside the workplace to where this generation does all of its daytime socialising and networking – the cafe. If you can get your Gen Y staff outside the office you stand a far better chance of developing a rapport and relationship that will lead to honesty. Without a level of rapport and trust, this group will just play the game, giving the answers and setting the goals that they think you want to hear.

Generation Ys have career expectations that could appear impetuous at best and presumptuous at worst. They honestly expect to make career advancements in the first 18 months and will leave organizations if they feel that a role is not continually challenging them. What is surprising to many managers and employers is that what represents career advancement for this group is not necessarily a pay rise or a promotion. Lateral moves and job rotations are good but they are not necessary to keep Gen Y engaged.

Consider the example of Jason, a marketing manager I worked with recently. Jason faced the challenge of engaging a Gen Y staff member (let's call her Annette) who worked in the market research section of his department. Annette indicated in the course of a quarterly performance dialogue that she was looking for a new position because she was 'bored'. Recognizing that this is the word that most commonly precedes emotional and then official resignation from Gen Y, Jason started by asking Annette what sort of skills she would like to develop outside her current position. Of course, Annette responded as most 22-year-olds would by saying that she didn't know. However, with some deliberate prompting and strategic questions, Jason discovered that Annette was actually keen to develop her sales and communication skills.

As is the case in most organizations, Jason recognized that a department transfer or job rotation was not going to be practical or possible and so he simply started giving Annette some targeted projects that forced her to move outside her comfort zone and interact more with clients. Over the next few months, Jason noticed the diligence and enthusiasm with which Annette approached these projects. She embraced the opportunity to develop new skills that were challenging and personally rewarding.

For managers like Jason, the key is first to listen to what it is that your Gen Y team members perceive as challenging and rewarding and then to assign projects and opportunities with this in mind. Be careful not to assume that you know what your staff want. Their goals and desires may be very different to your own and simply setting them goals that you would find challenging will be as effective as trying to sell ice to Eskimos. Tap into the desire first and then meet it if you want to motivate and keep your Gen Y staff.

Social researcher Mark McCrindle suggests that the secret to keeping Gen Y engaged is to offer wide job descriptions, varied work experiences and real opportunities for ongoing training and development. He cites one study which found that 90% of Gen Ys would stay with their current employer longer if their employer offered training.[111] In the same vein, he points to a similar study which showed that nearly 40% of Gen Y selected 'opportunity for advancement' as one of their top workplace needs.[112]

I came across one unique strategy for discovering what drives employees when recently working with a very forward-thinking organization. Recognizing the importance of finding out what motivated and interested their staff, this organization started conducting 'why do you stay here?' interviews with their employees. As opposed to the exit interviews many companies use when staff have announced their resignation, this organization initiated 'why do you stay here?' interviews in the belief that by being more proactive in understanding staff, they could design tasks and projects that keep employees challenged and engaged. In other words, they want to understand what their staff like about their job so they can give them more of it rather than waiting until staff resign and then asking why.

While many would argue that employees get paid to do the job they're doing and that should be reward enough, I would suggest that the more challenging you can make work for Gen Y through short-term goals and targeted projects, the more likely you are to motivate them and, more importantly, retain them.

15 CHAPTER FIFTEEN
USE STORIES TO
MAKE YOUR POINT

Seen in every culture, used throughout the centuries and understood from even the youngest age, stories are a powerful tool for teaching and learning. Great leaders in past eras have built empires, founded religions and inspired nations by the stories they have told.

Similarly, when it comes to engaging Gen Y, never underestimate the power of narrative. A postmodern generation is nowhere near as interested in whether something is *right* as they are in whether something *works*. The best way to show that a principle works is to place it in the context of experience – through stories.

In his book, *The Heart of Mentoring*, David Stoddard affirms this point: *Principles communicated through story have a far more profound effect on people and their lives than ideas presented outside the scope of human experience.*[113]

Stories connect with a postmodern mind-set because they illustrate a principle in action while leaving interpretation and personal application in the hands of the listener. Instead of dictating truth, you are simply illuminating a principle through experience and allowing the listener to attach their own meaning.

If you want to truly engage Generation Y you can no longer see yourself merely as a messenger delivering information. Your background, your history and your stories must become the centerpiece of your message. The old adage is true – the most significant lessons in life are better caught than taught. Teaching through narrative is the most effective way of helping young people to 'catch' the lesson you are trying to get through.

When I started speaking to Gen Y students my approach was to outline two or three ideas of content and then throw in a story for good measure. The general format of my sessions followed the familiar pattern of content/content/story. It didn't take me long to figure out, however, that this approach wasn't working. Students would switch off within ten minutes and

> "THE MOST SIGNIFICANT LESSONS IN LIFE ARE BETTER CAUGHT THAN TAUGHT."

getting them back became an almost impossible task. It seemed that no matter how many PowerPoint images and videos I used, the only thing they really listened to was the stories. Whenever I would start to tell a story the engagement and connection was palpable.

Recognizing this, I started to design my content around stories rather than my stories around content. The general format became: story/story/content. It worked! I started to elaborate on the stories by adding more color, more emotion, and more of myself. I found that even in the toughest schools, infamous for disinterested and disengaged students, I could spend an hour speaking to hundred 10th graders and have them entranced the whole time. Their teachers were astonished. They had never seen their students silent and attentive for more than two minutes, much less a whole hour.

The secret was simple – I became good at telling stories!

Good stories make an impact. They are memorable and fun. Even from your own perspective as an adult learner you probably know this to be true. Think back to a conference or seminar you have attended recently. If I asked you to recall one thing about each of the presentations you heard at that event, what would you remember? It probably wouldn't be the PowerPoint slide charting statistical trends nor the seven-point strategy that promised to solve all your problems. In most cases you probably wouldn't even be able to recall the name of the speaker.

What you are almost certain to remember is one or more of the stories that the presenters told. The young people you are aiming to connect with and inspire are no different.

Probably the best example I have seen of storytelling and narrative being used in the business world is in network marketing organizations I have presented to in recent years. Otherwise known as Multi Level Marketing, this style of organization relies heavily on relationships and a sense of empowered and shared vision. By

"WHILE YOUNG PEOPLE RESIST YOUR JUDGMENT, THEY ARE VERY INTERESTED IN YOUR JOURNEY."

deliberately sharing the stories and testimonials of leaders within these organizations, network marketing businesses achieve levels of motivation, commitment and enthusiasm that are rarely seen in the more traditional corporate arena. The power of storytelling in this context is that it captures real life experiences and gives a sense of hope that the example of another's success may provide a pattern or blueprint for your own.

While many companies tend to dismiss the role of organizational storytelling and narrative as too 'fluffy', they do so at their own peril. Sure the facts, the data and the research models may convince and persuade those you lead, but nothing will inspire and enthuse them like the experiences and stories of others who are seen to be 'just like them'. This is never truer than with a postmodern group like Gen Y. If you are an employer or business leader I urge you to create forums and space in your organizations for people to share their stories and experiences. Whether this is in a group setting, in online blogs or one on one over a coffee, these stories have the power to convey principles for success, efficiency and resilience like nothing else.

For parents, storytelling is equally important. You may have noticed how quickly your child will shut down when you give judgements and suggestions. The minute they feel that you are offering advice or directives, this group will disengage almost immediately. You may be surprised, however, to realize that while young people resist your *judgment*, they are very interested in your *journey*. They are fascinated by your stories – even if they don't show it. They love to hear what you did, why you did it, what you learned and what you would change if you had your time again.

If you want to encourage younger generations to persist in the face of setbacks and disappointments, be bold enough to share your experiences of what you have done when faced with hardships in life. While it is important to be sensitive and discerning when sharing experiences, your stories of either persevering or giving up in the face of adversity will speak volumes to Gen Y. It is true that in life we always pay either the price of discipline or regret and by you sharing your experiences of when you have paid one or the other, you are likely to encourage young people to make wise and informed decisions for themselves.

Whether it be regarding career choice, relationships, smoking, the traps of car finance, the importance of study or any number of other topics, try the approach of telling your son or daughter a story rather than simply offering advice. One of the challenges that many parents face in telling their stories is to find the appropriate time, context and tone to do so. If this is the case for you, start by writing your stories down. I make this suggestion because you may find that the moment your son or daughter is ready to listen to and learn from your stories occurs years or even decades after the moment you are ready, willing and able to share them. The tragedy is that only 4% of people ever take the time to sit down and record their stories. So often, we figure that we will get around to doing this one day but for too many people, that day never comes. The other challenge is knowing where to start. Recording the stories of your life can seem overwhelming and intimidating.

With this in mind, I recently released a gift book called **Memento.** Consisting of 130 carefully crafted questions, this journal-style book is designed to help parents capture the moments, memories, stories and experiences that have shaped who they are in order to pass these on as a handwritten legacy to the next generation. For more information on this book, visit **www.mementobook.com**.

Regardless of whether you write your stories down or would rather look for opportunities to share them in person, here are some suggestions and guidelines for communicating through narrative:

- **Be authentic and honest.** Embellishments, half-truths and a positive personal bias will alienate Gen Y. Share the truth, the whole truth and nothing but the truth, warts and all, for greatest effect. Also, be aware of the rose-colored glasses syndrome. Try to remember events and experiences exactly how they were for you at the time, not with the benefit of hindsight and selective memory.

- **Beware of sharing that is self-indulgent and self-serving.** Ask yourself if the story you are sharing is really designed to benefit the listener. If the purpose of the story is self-serving or designed simply to shock, impress or intimidate the listener, you will find that the narrative will be counterproductive in achieving cross-generational engagement.

- **Aim to promote growth of understanding for shared experience** not to manipulate or convince. If there is a hidden agenda to the story, young people will sense it a mile away and immediately develop distrust and suspicion.

- **Tell stories pre-emptively**. It is important to share stories that model a principle or lesson just before it will be needed by the recipient. This is particularly important for parents telling their teenage children stories designed to help their kids make wise choices at certain life stages. For example, sharing your experiences relating to binge drinking and drug use would be useful when your children are age 13 or 14. If you share the story much earlier than this age it will seem irrelevant but if you share it much later once experimentation may have already begun, it could come across as contrived or manipulative. Sharing a story and teaching a principle just before it is needed requires a degree of sensitivity and discernment on the part of the parent, teacher or employer. Planting the 'seed' of an impacting and timely narrative in the fertile soil of a young person who is ready to receive it is vital to the effectiveness of the story.

- **Be subtle and strategic.** Don't make a big deal out of sharing your stories but rather weave them into everyday conversations and life. Remember too that gender can have a huge influence on the effectiveness of communication. Boys tend be more able and willing to engage in conversation when side by side rather than face to face. As such, if you are sharing your stories or experiences with a son or younger male, try doing so while watching a sports match, fishing or driving in the car rather than over a coffee table.

- **Don't read your experience into someone else's.** Beware of the temptation to assume that you know how somebody else feels simply because your story or experience may be similar to theirs. Share your experience by all means but allow the listener to make the connection of commonality without pre-empting it.

- **Get to the point**. In using narrative to convey a principle or model an idea effectively, it is vital to use language that creates a mental image for the listener. The human brain thinks in pictures and so developing the scene, the emotion and the context of a story is all part of the art form. However, it is important that the *methods* of the narrative don't become the focus. When telling stories, be careful to make sure you get to the point relatively quickly while still making the journey one that interests, entertains and engages your audience by helping them touch, taste, feel and experience it.

If all this talk of telling your personal stories is a little uncomfortable, you may prefer to use the stories of history, people you have known, and even examples from contemporary popular culture. Whether the stories you tell are your own or not, you will find that narrative will be far more effective in communicating a principle or illuminating consequences than a well-worded sermon will ever be.

For teachers, you will be amazed at how interested your students are to hear about you, your life and your experiences. As we discussed in Chapter 9, the very fact that you are a real person with a real life and real stories will amaze them no end.

In the classroom, the stories you tell will go a long way towards creating memorable learning experiences for your students. Furthermore, sharing stories is a powerful means of building the authenticity and rapport that provides the foundation for an engaging relationship.

Beware, however, of falling into the trap of only telling the stories that paint you in your best light. As teachers, parents and managers, you have probably learned most from your mistakes. Likewise, the young people you are aiming to connect with will probably learn more from your shortcomings than your triumphs. Don't be afraid to share your stories of failure, weakness and humanness. Your successes may impress the younger generation but the stories that depict the real you will be the ones that truly impact them.

16

GO FOR COMMITMENT, NOT COMPLIANCE

In the mid 1800s, vast tracts of land in central Australia were granted to immigrants who had, in many cases, just arrived from Europe. These farmers and pastoralists found themselves with a challenge – they were now in control of expanses of land that were, in some cases, almost as large as the countries they had just come from.

Back in Europe, the farming methods of the day were tried and tested – buy a plot of land and build a fence around it. Next, put your stock on the land and then farm your stock. However, given the enormous outback properties, there were at least two reasons why this European approach to farming was not going to work in the Australian context. Firstly, to put a fence around these massive stations was going to cost a small fortune both to build and maintain. Secondly, the entire fence would be rendered useless if even a small section on a far-flung outpost of the property were to be compromised.

These farmers were clever enough to know that a new strategy was necessary. As they considered the different options for farming in this new country, it was Australia's climate that gave these pioneers a clue to the approach that would work best. In a land where water was scarce, farmers discovered that if they dug a watering hole or well in the middle of their properties there would never be any need to build a fence. To put it more simply, if the animals had a good enough reason to stay on the farm, the farmer would never have to worry about forcing them to stay.

When it comes to leading, teaching and raising Generation Y, I believe there are a number of lessons that teachers and parents can learn from this approach.

Gen Y has the reputation of being a generation of free agents – in other words, they have their own agenda, are unyielding and not collectivist by nature. Achieving cohesion and cooperation from a group of free agents could perhaps be described as a challenge akin to herding cats – not an easy task by any measure.

In leading this generation, what strategy do you use – fences or watering holes, compliance or commitment?

Compliance is all about rules, expectations and 'shoulds'. It places a great emphasis on obedience ('just because I said so') and falling into line. Process-driven institutions, such as the ones described in Chapter 11, tend to focus almost exclusively on compliance. Furthermore, compliance

COMPLIANCE IS ALL ABOUT RULES, EXPECTATIONS AND 'SHOULDS'.

is the yardstick of authority for managers and leaders who adopt a Power and Control mind-set as discussed in Chapter 9.

The problem with compliance is that it only gives two options – to comply or not to comply. Furthermore, using compliance as a model of managing human behavior is only as effective as the enforcing authority's ability to create fear. It also tends to stifle creativity, innovation and a sense of personal responsibility. Echoing this sentiment, sports psychologist and author Gavin

Freeman challenges business leaders to build a culture where people are motivated to succeed rather than motivated to avoid failure. The former is characterized by a positive drive to innovate, achieve and improve, while the latter tends to be a fear-driven compulsion to not fail, make a mistake or get caught out.

Like every generation of teenagers before them, Generation Y doesn't respond well to compliance. Upon encountering a fence, their first and natural response is to ask 'Why is it there?' More often than not, this is met with a non-response that invalidates the question and infuriates the questioner.

The result is a chain of events that most parents and teachers will easily be able to relate to: the young person attempts to find a way over, under or around the fence, or alternatively gets all their friends together to help them knock the fence down. Incensed by such blatant disrespect and

COMMITMENT IS CHARACTERIZED BY OPPORTUNITY, BUY-IN, MOTIVATORS AND OUTCOMES.

insubordination, those in authority build the fence longer, stronger and higher in an effort to make sure that their power and control is not threatened. Teachers shout louder, children are grounded yet again, written warnings are given and privileges are removed.

An icy standoff ensues. Distrust, frustration and anger create a climate where cooperation, engagement and relationship seem like the unattainable dream.

Does this story sound familiar?

If so, maybe it's time to try digging a well rather than building another fence – to go for commitment rather than compliance.

Commitment is characterized by opportunity, buy-in, motivators and outcomes. It is cause-driven and offers a reason *why* a young person would respond rather than simply dictating *what* is expected in terms of behavior, action and response.

If you are going to go for commitment over compliance, the first key is to respond well to the classic question of 'why' from this generation. Rather than responding to it defensively by reinforcing your power and authority, try viewing this question as an opportunity to give your students and children a reason to commit.

While this may all sound very nice in theory, you may be wondering how a 'commitment' approach could work in the real world. Consider the following examples.

A few years ago I was speaking at a parents' conference on the challenge of Engaging Gen Y at Home. During the lunch break I was approached by a woman who introduced herself and thanked me for the session I had just delivered. We chatted briefly about the weather and the food, but I sensed there was something specific that she wanted to ask me. Within minutes it became clear.

She started out by saying, 'Can you tell me what to do with my lazy son?' At this point I knew I should tread carefully and so I started asking her some questions to clarify exactly what she meant.

She explained, 'My son has been offered a job at Coles. He has had the interview and has been given the job. There's just one last thing that he has to do before he can start work.'

'What's that?' I inquired.

'He has to fill out the 8-page exam before they will process his application and give him his first shift. His interview was over four weeks ago but he *still* hasn't bothered to sit down for half an hour and complete the exam paper. I've tried everything to make him do it but he simply won't. What should I do?'

I am always hesitant to give simple answers in situations such as these, so I did the safest thing – I asked more questions. 'What have you tried doing so far?'

'Well, every day I keep telling him to get his butt into gear and do the exam. I have even taken away some of his privileges, like X-Box time, until he does the exam. Still, he won't do it.'

I tried a different approach. 'What happens if he does get this job?'

She thought for a moment but said nothing.

I continued. 'More to the point, what is the consequence of his not getting this job?' I paused to let her think for a few seconds – I could tell that a moment of realization had just taken place.

'Ah ha!' she said. 'I know why he hasn't bothered to do the exam – he doesn't need the money badly enough'.

She went on to tell me how she pays for her son's cell phone, car payment, gas and living expenses. It's no wonder he wasn't in a rush to start working – I wouldn't be either! This newly inspired mother went home that day, resolved not to pay her son's way any longer. Poor kid – some teenager out there probably resents me for instantly making his life a lot harder!

I don't know what developed in the weeks and months following that conversation. I imagine, however, that this woman's son became very proactive about earning an income once the tap was turned off. As soon as there was a reason to act, a motivation to get moving, I bet he completed that application form in record time.

This mother, like so many parents I speak with, had seemingly tried everything. Persistent nagging hadn't worked. Even withholding privileges hadn't worked. In fact, all that those things had represented was the big fence of compliance. What her son needed was a reason WHY.

The essence of human motivation is that we act in response to one of two desires: either to avoid pain or move toward pleasure. While both these motivators can work in bringing about behavioral change, the biggest drawback with the compliance approach is that it tends to focus exclusively on the avoidance of manufactured and regulated pain. To this end, it relies heavily upon negative reinforcement, punishment and the removal of benefits to bring about obedience – all things that stifle, contain and eventually crush the human spirit. The challenge for parents and teachers, then, is to move beyond merely focussing on the negative consequences of non-compliance and instead to emphasize the positive benefits of the desired response.

> "IF YOU ARE GOING TO GIVE THIS GENERATION SOMETHING TO COMMIT TO, YOU NEED TO APPEAL TO BOTH THEIR NOBLE AND THEIR SELFISH SIDES."

If you can shift your focus from compliance to commitment in this way, you'll undoubtedly find that young people respond with a greater willingness than if you simply crack the rule-driven whip of 'should' and 'must'. In other words, you need to find creative ways to answer the all-important question at the heart of all human drive: *What's in it for me?* Whether this is through rewards that are linked to the attainment of a goal, or by casting the vision of a favorable outcome, the subtle difference between going for commitment rather than compliance may be as simple as changing the language, emphasis and tone used to bring about behavioral change.

In thinking of how this scenario could play out in a classroom setting, I recalled a recent conversation with a science teacher who told me how he had made use of the commitment approach to working with a 'problem child' in one of his classes. For one reason or another, this particular student (let's call him John) felt he was exempt from the school rule that required students to leave their bags outside the science lab on their way into the room. The teacher I was speaking with responded as most teachers would. He stated the rules and demanded the student's compliance with only limited and short-term effect. John would take his bag out as he was told only to bring it in with him again next lesson. Regardless of how many times he was asked and how many detentions he was given, John was simply not responding to the tools of compliance.

After weeks of frustration at the lack of response, the teacher tried a different tactic – going for commitment. Recognizing that John and the rest of his peers actually enjoyed science and loved doing the experiments, the teacher simply commenced a lesson one day by saying that there would be no experiments from now on unless all students left their bags at the door before entering the classroom. John of course was torn. As much as he wanted to dance to his own tune when it came to obeying school rules, he wanted to do the experiments too. What's more, his decision would have ramifications not just for him personally, but for his classmates and peers as well.

It only took one lesson for John to change his behavior and attitude. From the next lesson onwards, John left his bag outside the room without being asked. Where demanding compliance had not worked, getting John to commit to a certain course of action had led to real behavioral change.

To look further at how a commitment approach may work at a broader level, consider the case of a school principal I worked with recently who was facing a common challenge in student discipline. This principal spoke with pride of the school's relaxed atmosphere – teachers and students were open with each other and related well. Clearly, this principal was doing a lot of things right – the students' level of classroom engagement was evidence of this fact.

His challenge was that their school, like many others, has an assembly each Tuesday morning that all students are expected to attend. In recent times, however, a culture had developed at the school where students did not bother turning up for assembly. Over the past few years, the problem had escalated to the point where an overwhelming majority of students missed each assembly and turned up late to school. This open defiance of school rules, he said, was creating problems for teachers and other students and needed to be addressed.

'How do I get students to turn up like we require them to?' he asked.

As always, I responded with a question: 'Well let's look at that. Firstly, what is the purpose of your school assemblies?'

He seemed taken aback by this question. 'Well, we have always had them. They are part of the school timetable and it is something that we, as an executive, feel is important.'

I pressed a little further. 'From a student's perspective, what is the negative consequence of not coming to assembly?'

'Nothing, really,' he said. 'We can hardly give two thirds of the school population a lunchtime detention each week!'

'On the flip side then, what is the benefit of a student actually coming to assembly?' I asked.

'There is none, I guess,' he said.

I made an observation. 'So, in effect, you are telling your students that they must attend school assemblies that have no specific purpose, to receive no particular benefit, and face no real consequences if they fail to comply. In other words, come to assembly because you *should*.'

'Well, when you put it that way, yes,' he laughed.

'Can you see how all you have done is build fences of compliance around assemblies for your students?' I asked.

'Absolutely,' he said, finally realising. 'So, how do I dig a well – how do I give them something to commit to?'

We went on to speak for over 20 minutes about the paradoxical nature of motivating Generation Y. I explained that if you are going to give this generation something to commit to, you need to appeal to both their noble *and* their selfish sides.

As we have discussed in previous sections, this group is a civic-minded generation. They are volunteering at surprisingly high rates and have an innate sense of honor, respect and fairness. The paradox, however, is that this is also the most selfish and individualistic generation in living memory. The challenge in leading this group toward commitment is to appeal to both these sides of their psyche.

As this principal and I discussed the idea further, we came up with a number of strategies which would do just that.

In appealing to their selfish side, we agreed that the important key was to answer the *'What's in it for me?'* question. There had to be clearly communicated benefits to coming along to an assembly that those who didn't attend would miss out on. It could be information, opportunities or even attendance-based rewards that represented some tangible benefit to the student.

When it came to thinking of ways to appeal to their noble side the strategies took a bit more creativity. We talked about the idea of taking the students' focus off attending assembly for their own or their teacher's sake, and placing the emphasis on attending for their peers' sake. For example, perhaps at a certain assembly a number of students are going to be recognized for an achievement in sport. On this occasion, the approach could be to communicate to students that to be deliberately absent from that particular assembly would show a lack of respect and honor for their friends and fellow students. Furthermore, it would be unfair, as they would want to have their peers there if it were them receiving the recognition.

To broaden the noble appeal further, I encouraged this principal to try motivating a desired outcome from students by linking it to a cause and giving the students a level of responsibility and ownership. You only have to look at the way this generation have rallied around causes like the 'Make Poverty History' campaign and the 'Live Earth' concerts to see how powerful this motivator can be. They love to get behind an inspiring vision, and involve themselves in organizations, programs and initiatives that allow them to feel a part of something bigger than themselves.

One excellent example of using this approach to utilizing Gen Y's sense of civic duty is in Father Chris Riley's use of Service Learning with marginalized and homeless youth. Through his work as the founder of the well-known Australian charity *Youth Off The Streets*, Father Riley has had astonishing success in making inroads with disengaged young people. Speaking at a conference with Father Riley a number of months ago, I had the opportunity to hear him describe why Service Learning is such a key element of the program his organization runs.[114]

Defined as 'a method of instruction in which youth learn and develop through service participation in thoughtfully designed experiences', Service Learning is a powerful way to give young people a sense of achievement, ownership and responsibility. In a nutshell, Service Learning gives young people a way to feel involved in meeting an actual community need. Be it distributing goods to the poor, mowing lawns for elderly community members or raising money for breast cancer research, give Gen Y a cause to work towards and watch them come into their own.

This younger generation want to make a difference. If you can show them how they can do so by servicing a need and affecting change in the world around them, you will be amazed the impact this has on their sense of cohesion and commitment.

While going for commitment over compliance does take time, energy, patience and creativity, you will undoubtedly find it infinitely more effective in creating lasting change in the young people you lead.

Conclusion

As I have travelled around the globe speaking to audiences about the challenge of engaging Generation Y, I hear the same sentiments being expressed time and again.

Teachers are frustrated. Many educators feel it is futile trying to engage students who don't seem to be interested in learning. They tell me of the exasperation they feel when students quit on themselves, don't bring back permission slips and scoff at lessons which took hours of preparation time and a great deal of energy to create.

Similarly, parents are confused. In many cases, they feel as if they have failed. 'Why is it so difficult to connect with my son or daughter?' they ask. 'Am I doing something wrong?' These parents also express concern at the apparent disrespect and impatience of a generation who want everything handed to them on a plate.

Finally, employers and business owners are often irritated with a group who seem so aware of their rights and yet so unaware of their responsibilities. They talk of a generation who want everything now and are not willing to do the hard yards they themselves did in the early years of their career. However, these same employers are torn. They recognize the commercial benefits of employing this tech-savvy, well-educated group of confident, natural networkers.

Furthermore, they understand the market realities and the need to engage and retain talented Gen Y staff lest they leave to go and work for the competition.

And yet, despite the reputation that Generation Y has for being brash, self-confident, self-reliant and sometimes arrogant, I have had the opportunity through my work with this group to see behind the tough facade they often put up and what I have discovered is quite different to what you might expect.

Sure, Generation Y hide behind an often intimidating exterior. However, behind that wall this is a group who are desperately looking for leadership, boundaries and mentoring. With as many as 62% of Gen Y growing up without the presence of their biological father, the stereotype is sadly true – they are often a fatherless generation.[115]

Desperate for solid role models, Gen Y are seeking connection with adults who will relate to them and model what an authentic life looks like.

The worrying fact is that this generation is often not finding engagement from the adults around them. At home, they may not be connecting with their parents, either because modern life is so busy, or because the generation gap has become so wide that parents don't know where to start.

Then this group goes to school only to find teachers who are so stretched and pressured that the relationships and connections are not happening there either. Finally they go to work. Many times, however, they find no greater connection with their boss than they did with their teachers and parents. So who is Generation Y looking to for leadership, boundaries and mentoring? You guessed it... advertisers and the architects of popular culture.

If you are a parent of this generation, you may find it sobering to learn that advertisers are investing tens of billions of dollars each year around the world to better understand your children. And they do this with good reason. Author and media commentator, Douglas Rushkoff, quoted industry figures from 2006 which show that American Gen Ys had a combined buying power of over $100 billion.[116] The youth market is lucrative and advertisers know it.

These advertisers are, as Rushkoff describes them, 'merchants of cool'. That is, after all, what they are selling this generation – cool.

I for one don't want the next generation to be led through, given boundaries and mentoring by Paris Hilton and Pepsi. Do you? The reality is that if you as an adult are not connecting with this generation then that is who they are going to look to.

As a teacher, a parent or a business leader, the role you have to play has never been more important. Beyond the learning outcomes, the more harmonious functioning of households and the commercial gains of businesses, the part you play as an adult in engaging Generation Y is critical.

This role carries with it a great power and an incredible privilege that is often overlooked – the privilege of influence.

Regardless of whether you are the parent of one young person, a teacher of hundreds or an employer and leader of thousands, you have been given an amazing opportunity to guide and influence the next generation.

Try to remember this every time you interact with *your* young people. Whether around the kitchen table, in the classroom, or on a daily basis at work, you are helping to shape the next generation's potential and our society's future. Who knows, the throwaway comment you make next Thursday morning might just land in a young person's mind and start to make them think. What if that comment changes the way they view themselves and their future? What if it causes them to make a choice that alters the entire direction of their lives? What if that comment changes the way they raise their children? Now your influence has extended to a generation you will never meet! This is the privilege and opportunity that you have been given.

My sincere hope is that what you have learned in these pages will help you be an adult who truly engages with Generation Y. They are looking for connection and leadership – may you be someone in whom they can find these two things.

This is no easy task but it is possible and it is in every way worth it.

IF YOU WOULD LIKE TO BOOK **MICHAEL MCQUEEN** TO SPEAK AT YOUR NEXT CONFERENCE OR TRAINING EVENT, PLEASE

VISIT

www.TheNexgenGroup.com

HERE'S WHAT OTHERS HAVE SAID:

'Michael's presentation is both engaging and inspiring. With a predominantly Gen X leadership team, hearing Michael's strategies for engaging our Gen Y people really hit the mark. His presentation received such rave reviews, we've asked him back for another 3 presentations.'

Vanessa Riley, Head of Career & Development Vodafone Australia

'What an engaging, entertaining and well prepared session – the best generational presentation I've seen! Michael's depth of knowledge and applicable stories were fantastic.'

Robyn Quinn, Marketing Manager, Pepsi Australia

'Michael McQueen offers a fascinating and entertaining insight into the modern generation of young people. His fact-filled presentation would be of great benefit to parents, teachers, policy makers, marketers and business leaders.'

Liam King, Deputy Principal, The Australian International School, Singapore

'This session made me realize the importance of understanding all the generations in the workplace.'

Donna Green, Myer

'Michael McQueen is a presenter with the WOW factor. His insight into the thinking of Generation Y and his ability to contrast that with prior generations was uncanny and left our Rotary District Conference attendees wanting more. I commend him to any organization that wants to better understand its future employees and members.'

Greg Bailey, District Governor, Rotary District 9570

'Michael McQueen's presentations are brilliant. He is an informative and compelling speaker and his insights and wise advice for parents of teenagers are highly relevant.'

Prof. David Bennett, Head of Adolescent Medicine, Westmead Children's Hospital

'Michael is a gifted speaker with an enthralling topic. Colleagues and clients alike found Michael captivating and took away many lessons.'

Brett Duff - GIO Insurance

'Thank you for your presentation at the 2008 Sydney Regional Principals Conference. Your presentation, delivery and message were perfectly aligned with the conference theme.'

Dr Phil Lambert, Director Sydney Region Department of Education and Training

'What a helpful and informative session! You re-enforced a lot of the behaviors we are already seeing in our Gen Y staff and have given us some excellent strategies for how to better manage them. Thanks Michael.'

Annie Heetel, Operations Director, Lenovo Australia/New Zealand

'Understanding what makes Gens X & Y tick is not a new challenge which is why Michael McQueen's presentation of his findings were unexpectedly refreshing. Our delegates responded with knowing nods and had many a light bulb moments throughout his session. Michael is a fluid and mature presenter who is completely across his subject.'

Philippa Taylor, CEO, Family Business Australia

'Thank you Michael for your presentation at our recent Chamber breakfast. I was totally captivated by the information you gave us in a short time and this has helped me immensely to better understand and establish relationships with the many young people I deal with in the workplace. I bought your book and can't put it down! Thanks again.'

Kim Robinson, Devonport Chamber of Commerce & Industry

'This evening's session was so enjoyable, informative and engaging. As a teacher and a parent, you have given me some great hints, suggestions and practical strategies for working with young people.'

Ann Bloomfield, Parent

'Thanks Michael for your fantastic session at our recent conference. I have worked with a lot of speakers and you are definitely a stand out. Some speakers twice your age charge twice as much and deliver only half of the value you do. I wouldn't hesitate in recommending you to anyone.'

Sara Mitchell, Group Training Australia

'Congratulations Michael and thank you again for your recent presentation at the Killara High School Executive Conference. You challenged our collective mindset and engaged all 19 of my highly experienced and talented executive colleagues – no mean feat in itself.'

Mark Carter, Principal, Killara High School

'Thank you for your opening keynote presentation at the 2007 NSW PDHPE Teachers Association Conference. The number of delegates who spoke to me about how valuable both your session and workshop were was simply amazing. You created a sensational buzz from the start of the conference and this did not disappear.'

Ellie Donovan, NSW 2007 PDHPE Conference Chairperson

'Michael's presentation at our recent business breakfast was enlightening and entertaining. I have received very positive feedback from the participants and some of them said they could have listened to Michael all day.'

Leonie Kennedy, NSW Business Chamber

'What a vibrant, engaging and enlightening session! As a parent of a Gen Y and step-parent of a Gen X, you have really helped me to understand myself and my children far better.'

Karen Womersley, Parent

'Michael's presentation was bright, easy to listen to and very relevant. It gave me a greater appreciation of how young minds work.'

Peter Conroy, Deputy Principal, Mount View High School

'Michael was excellent. His session was an outstanding awakening for a baby boomer like me!'

Ian Skilton, Deputy Principal, Singleton High School

'Sensational! Michael is an excellent speaker and has given me some genuine insights and strategies for better communicating with my daughter.'

Kate Fitzallen, Parent

'Fantastic! Every teacher of people 14–19 years old would benefit from the clear frameworks and deep insights in this presentation. A teacher's 'must do'.'

J Dickins, CGVE Teacher, Randwick TAFE

BIBLIOGRAPHY

1. Nader, C 2003, *'Generation Y: complex, discerning and suspicious.'* The Age, 9 October.
2. Chatzky, J 1999, *'Young, rich, smart.'* USA Weekend, 2 May
3. Codrington, G & Grant-Marshall, S 2004, *Mind the Gap*, Penguin Books, South Africa, p. 11.
4. Kohlberg , L 1983, *Moral stages: a current formulation and a response to critics*, Karger, Switzerland.
5. Davis, M 1997, *Gangland: Cultural Elites and the New Generationalism*, Allen and Unwin, Australia.
6. Plotz, D 1999, *'The American Teen-ager: Why Generation Y?'* Slate, 17 September.
7. Elmore, T 2010, *Generation iY*, Poet Gardener, Atlanta, p. 142.
8. McCrindle, M 2009, *The ABC of XYZ*, UNSW Press, Australia, p. 4.
9. Codrington, G & Grant-Marshall S 2004, *Mind the Gap*, Penguin Books, South Africa, p. 27.
10. Jones, L 1980, *Great Expectations: America and the Baby Boom Generation*, Coward, McCann, New York.
11. *Television History – The First 75 Years*, 'Number of TV Households in America' <http://www.tvhistory.tv>
12. Codrington, G & Grant-Marshall, S 2004, *Mind the Gap*, Penguin Books, South Africa, p. 40.
13. 2009, *The Baby Boomers, The US Economic Collapse and the Future of Senior Housing* <http://www.articlesbase.com/elderly-carearticles/baby-boomers-the-u-s-economic-collapse-and-the-future-ofsenior-housing-793538.html> Accessed 12 January 2011.
14. Doughty, S 2009, *'80% of UK's wealth belongs to the over 50s.'* The Daily Mail, 6 April.

15. Weintraub, A 2006, 'Selling The Promise Of Youth.' *BusinessWeek*, 20 March.

16. David, G 2002, *'Aren't You Boomers Ever Going Away?'* Fortune Magazine, 7 January.

17. Codrington, G & Grant-Marshall, S 2004, *Mind the Gap*, Penguin Books, South Africa, p. 49.

18. McCrindle, M 2009, *The ABC of XYZ*, UNSW Press, Australia p. 61.

19. Elkind, D 1998, *All Grown Up and No Place To Go: Teenagers in Crisis*, Da Capo Press, New York.

20. Codrington, G & Grant-Marshall, S 2004, *Mind the Gap*, Penguin Books, South Africa, 2004, p. 50.

21. Hurd, G & Ashton DN 1986, *Human Societies: an Introduction to Sociology*, Routledge, New York, p. 207.

22. Codrington, G & Grant-Marshall, S 2004, *Mind the Gap*, Penguin Books, South Africa, p. 49.

23. Ibid, p. 52.

24. Isaacs, J et al. 2008, *Getting Ahead or Losing Ground: Economic Mobility in America*, The Brookings Institution.

25. Stephey, M. J. 2008, 'Gen-X: The Ignored Generation?' *Time Magazine*, 16 April.

26. McCrindle, M 2009, *The ABC of XYZ*, UNSW Press, Australia, p. 28.

27. Elmore, T 2010, *Generation iY*, Poet Gardener, Atlanta, p. 139.

28. Codrington, G & Grant-Marshall, S 2004, *Mind the Gap*, Penguin Books, South Africa, p. 50.

29. Howe, N & Strauss, W 2000, *Millennials Rising*, Vintage Books, New York, pp. 123–142.

30. Twenge, J 2006, *Generation Me*, Free Press, New York, p. 53.

31. Ibid, p. 66.

32. Elmore, T 2010, *Generation iY*, Poet Gardener, Atlanta, p. 41.

33. Twenge, J 2006, *Generation Me*, Free Press, New York, p. 241.

34. Jayson, S 2006, *'Generation Y gets involved'* USA Today, 23 October.

35. Elmore, T 2010, *Generation iY*, Poet Gardener, Atlanta p. 133.

36. Quindlen, A 2000, *'Now It's Time For Generation Next.'* Newsweek, 1 January.

37. Tapscott, D, 2009, *Grown Up Digital*, McGraw Hill, New York, p. 32.

38. Ibid, p. 238.

39. Ibid, p. 289.

40. Chester, E 2002, *Employing Generation Why?* Tucker House Books, Lakewood, CO, pp. 14–15.

41. Tapscott, D, 2009, *Grown Up Digital*, McGraw Hill, New York, p. 239.

42. McCrindle, M 2009, *The ABC of XYZ*, UNSW Press, Australia p. 81.

43. Louv, R 2005, *Last Child in the Woods*, Algonquin Books, North Carolina, p. 34.

44. LeClaire, J 2006, *'Kids and Tech: How Much Is Too Much?'* TechNewsWorld, 9 June.

45. McCrindle, M 2009, *The ABC of XYZ*, UNSW Press, Australia, p. 66.

46. Elmore, T 2010, *Generation iY*, Poet Gardener, Atlanta, p. 63..

47. Elmore, T 2010, *Generation iY*, Poet Gardener, Atlanta, p. 63

48. McCrindle, M 2009, *The ABC of XYZ*, UNSW Press, Australia, p. 83.

49. Grose, M 2005, *XYZ: The New Rules of Generational Warfare*, Random House, Australia, p. 38.

50. MacKay, H 2008, *'Kids' parties, teeny-raunch and other adult pursuits.'* Sydney Morning Herald, 12 January.

51. Tapscott, D, 2009, *Grown Up Digital*, McGraw Hill, New York, p. 224.

52. Twenge, J 2006, *Generation Me*, Free Press, New York, p. 75.

53. Masters, C 2007, *'Boring playgrounds deprive kids.'* The Daily Telegraph, 26 June.

54. Skenazy, L 2009, *Free Range Kids*, Jossey-Bass, San Francisco, p. xiii.

55. McCrindle, M 2009, *The ABC of XYZ*, UNSW Press, Australia, p. 87.

56. Tapscott, D, 2009, *Grown Up Digital*, McGraw Hill, New York, p. 222.

57. Louv, R 2005, *Last Child in the Woods*, Algonquin Books, North Carolina, p. 127.

58. Elmore, T 2010, *Generation iY*, Poet Gardener, Atlanta, p. 95.

59. Skenazy, L 2009, *Free Range Kids*, Jossey-Bass, San Francisco, p. 45.

60. McCrindle, M 2009, *The ABC of XYZ*, UNSW Press, Australia, p.22.

61. Ibid, p. 67.

62. Twenge, J 2006, *Generation Me*, Free Press, New York, p 28.

63. Hicks, R & K 1999, *Boomers, Xers and Other Strangers*, Tyndale House Publishers, Wheaton IL, pp. 326, 327.

64. Twenge, J 2006, *Generation Me*, Free Press, New York, p. 27.

65. McCrindle, M 2009, *The ABC of XYZ*, UNSW Press, Australia, p. 93.

66. Tapscott, D, 2009, *Grown Up Digital*, McGraw Hill, New York, p. 46.

67. McCrindle, M 2009, *The ABC of XYZ*, UNSW Press, Australia p. 157.

68. This text was adapted from the widely quoted opening sentence of a school essay submitted in 2002 by a 13-year old Scottish student

69. Preston, M 2007, *'Who'd hire a Gen-Y?'* Smartcompany, 12 July.

70. McCrindle, M 2009, *The ABC of XYZ*, UNSW Press, Australia, p. 157.

71. Elmore, T 2010, *Generation iY*, Poet Gardener, Atlanta, p. 33.

72. Ibid, p. 34.

73. Corderoy, A 2010, *'Lack of sleep linked to mental illness.'* Sydney Morning Herald, 1 September.

74. Twenge, J 2006, *Generation Me*, Free Press, New York, p. 234.

75. Elmore, T 2010, *Generation iY*, Poet Gardener, Atlanta, p. 47.

76. Laing, A 2010, *'Teenagers only use 800 different words a day.'* The Telegraph, 11 January.

77. Tapscott, D, 2009, *Grown Up Digital*, McGraw Hill, New York, p. 167.

78. Twenge, J 2006, *Generation Me*, Free Press, New York, p. 69.

79. Elmore, T 2010, *Generation iY*, Poet Gardener, Atlanta, p. 46.

80. Ball, C 2008, *'Technological Support: Making information systems work for you.'* The Meeting Professional, January.

81. Stern, L 2009, *'The New American Job: Are freelance and part-time gigs the future?'* Newsweek, 28 January.

82. McCrindle, M 2009, *The ABC of XYZ*, UNSW Press, Australia, p.133

83. Tapscott, D, 2009, *Grown Up Digital*, McGraw Hill, New York, p. 74.

84. Warner, J, 2010, *'The Why-Worry Generation'* The New York Times, 24 May.

85. Martin, C & Tuglan, B 2001, *Managing Generation Y*, HRD Press, Amherst MA, pp 51-62.

86. Tapscott, D, 2009, *Grown Up Digital*, McGraw Hill, New York, p. 106.

87. Simon, A 2005, *'The New Modus Operandi: Techno Tasking.'* The School Administrator April.

88. Tapscott, D, 2009, *Grown Up Digital*, McGraw Hill, New York, p. 100.

89. Richtel, M, 2010, *'Growing Up Digital, Wired For Distraction'* The New York Times, 21 November.

90. McCrindle, M 2009, *The ABC of XYZ*, UNSW Press, Australia, p. 110.

91. Dretzin, R & Rushkoff, D 2010, *'Digital Nation'* Frontline PBS Special. 2 February.

92. Tapscott, D, 2009, *Grown Up Digital*, McGraw Hill, New York, p. 3.

93. Ibid, p. 108.

94. Ibid, p. 98.

95. Ibid, p. 107.

96. McCrindle, M 2009, *The ABC of XYZ*, UNSW Press, Australia, p. 171.

97. Elmore, T 2010, *Generation iY*, Poet Gardener, Atlanta, p.104.

98. Codrington, G & Grant-Marshall, S 2004, *Mind the Gap*, Penguin Books, South Africa, p 120

99. Tapscott, D, 2009, *Grown Up Digital*, McGraw Hill, New York, p. 74.

100. Erwin, P 2008, 'Companies that will hire you to work at home' *CNN. com/Living*, 1 December.

101. Bai, M 2007, '*Home-Office Politics*' The New York Times, 4 November.

102. Frangipane, F 2002, *Becoming Unoffendable*, Lutheran Renewal.

103. Tapscott, D, 2009, *Grown Up Digital*, McGraw Hill, New York, p. 169.

104. Vogt, Brown & Isaacs 2003, *The Art of Powerful Questions*, Whole Systems Associates, Norfolk VA.

105. Riestenberg, N 2002, '*Restorative measures in schools: Evaluation results.*' Paper presented at the Third International Conference on Conferencing, Circles and other Restorative Practices, Minneapolis, August.

106. Zaslow, J 2007, '*Most-Praised Generation Craves Kudos at the Office.*' Wall Street Journal, April.

107. Blanchard, K et al. 2002, *Whale Done: The Power of Positive Relationships*, Free Press, New York.

108. Twenge, J 2006, *Generation Me*, Free Press, New York, p. 110.

109. Elmore, T 2010, *Generation iY*, Poet Gardener, Atlanta, p. 119.

110. Reh, FJ 2009, '*How To Give Negative Feedback Properly*' from About. com, April.

111. McCrindle, M 2009, *The ABC of XYZ*, UNSW Press, Australia, p. 134.

112. Ibid p 144

113. Stoddard, D 2003, *The Heart of Mentoring*, NavPress Books, Colorado Springs, p. 24.

114. For more information visit www.youthoffthestreets.com.au/ teachingunits/

115. Elmore, T 2010, *Generation iY*, Poet Gardener, Atlanta, p. 56.

116. Rushkoff, D 2001, '*The Merchants of Cool*' Frontline PBS Special. 27 February.

IF YOU ARE INTERESTED IN READING MORE ABOUT CONNECTING GENERATIONS, THE FOLLOWING BOOKS ARE A GOOD PLACE TO START:

Cohen, Norman 1999 *The Managers Pocket Guide to Effective* (Mentoring. HRD Press)

Cork, David 1998 *The Pig and the Python: How to Prosper From the Aging Baby Boom.* (Prima Publishing)

Egeler, Daniel 2003 *Mentoring Millennials: Shaping the Next Generation.* (NavPress)

Lancaster, Lynne & Stillman, David 2002 *When Generations Collide.* (HarperCollins Publishers)

Martin, Carolyn & Tuglan, Bruce 2001 *Managing Generation Y.* (Rainmaker Thinking)

Martin Carolyn & Tuglan, Bruce 2002 *Managing the Generational Mix* (HRD Press)

Murray, Margo 2001 *Beyond the Myths and Magic of Mentoring* (John Wiley & Sons)

Raines, Claire 1997 *Beyond Generation X: A Practical Guide for Managers.* (Crisp Publications)

Raines, Claire 2003 *Connecting Generations: The sourcebook for a new workplace.* (Crisp Publications)

Sheahan, Peter 2005 *Generation Y: Thriving and Surviving with Generation Y at Work.* (Hardie Grant Books)

Tuglan, Bruce 1996 *Managing Generation X.* (WW Norton & Company)

Zoba, Wendy 1999 *Generation 2K: What parents and others need to know about the Millennials.* (Intervarsity Press)